British Political Ideologi

CONTEMPORARY POLITICAL STUDIES

Series Editor: John Benyon, Director,
Centre for the Study of Public Order, University of Leicester

A series which provides authoritative yet concise introductory
accounts of key topics in contemporary political studies.

Other titles in the series include:

Elections and Voting Behaviour in Britain
David Denver, University of Lancaster

Pressure Groups, Politics and Democracy in Britain
Wyn Grant, University of Warwick

UK Political Parties since 1945
Edited by Anthony Seldon, Institute of Contemporary British
History

Politics and Policy Making in Northern Ireland
Michael Connolly, University of Ulster

Local Government and Politics in Britain
John Kingdom, Sheffield City Polytechnic

CONTEMPORARY POLITICAL STUDIES

British Political Ideologies

ROBERT LEACH
Leeds Polytechnic

Philip Allan
NEW YORK   LONDON   TORONTO   SYDNEY   TOKYO   SINGAPORE

First published 1991 by
Philip Alan
66 Wood Lane End, Hemel Hempstead
Hertfordshire, HP2 4RG
A division of
Simon & Schuster International Group

Typeset in 10/12pt Times by
Keyboard Services, Luton, Beds

Printed and bound in Great Britain by
Biddles Ltd, Guildford and King's Lynn

British Library Cataloguing in Publication Data

Leach, Robert
 British political ideologies. – (Contemporary political
 studies series).
 1. Great Britain. Political ideologies
 I. Title   II. Series
 320.50941

 ISBN 0–86003–868–8
 ISBN 0–86003–869–6 pbk

4 5   95 94 93

Contents

Preface

This book provides a simple introduction to the extremely complex and controversial subject of British political ideologies. It is intended primarily for both undergraduates and A level students, although hopefully it will also interest any intelligent layperson who desires to know more about liberalism, socialism, conservatism and other political creeds.

The scope and breadth of the book inevitably requires a somewhat brief and perhaps over-simplified treatment of great themes and complex ideas. Moreover, although I have tried to be as dispassionate and detached as possible in discussing a wide range of sharply opposed viewpoints, it is only too likely that my interpretation of some ideologies will be seen as partial or narrow. I can only repeat that this book is intended as an introductory text. Those who seek further illumination are advised to delve more deeply into the extensive literature on political ideas, some of which is indicated in the bibliography.

I would like to thank John Benyon, the series editor, and Clare Grist of Philip Allan for their help and advice. Several colleagues at Leeds Polytechnic have read part of the manuscript, and I would like to thank in particular Brendan Sheehan and Janie Percy-Smith for their detailed and constructive advice. I also owe a debt to my students, particularly on the BA Economics and Public Policy degree, for sharpening my ideas.

I would also like to acknowledge a few longer-term debts – to my late mother, and my father, for the support they gave to my education, and my shifting, eccentric academic pursuits, and to my old history teacher, Michael Cherniavsky, who first stimulated my interest in political ideas and much else besides. My greatest debt is, however, to my wife, Judith, without whose constant encouragement and support this book would certainly never have been written.

1

Ideology

The end of ideology?

In 1960 Daniel Bell confidently proclaimed the 'end of ideology'.
This scarcely involved a revolution in thinking about politics, more
confirmation of a trend which was already well under way. Political
ideologies seemed at best irrelevant, at worst positively dangerous
in the post-war western world. Between the wars Europe had been
an ideological battleground as the rival creeds of communism and
fascism contended for supremacy. The defeat and discrediting of
fascism, and the excesses of Stalinism provoked a reaction against
what were now lumped together as 'totalitarian' ideologies (Arendt,
1967; Talmon, 1960). Moreover, the very term 'ideology', which
had always had rather ambivalent connotations, was also substantially discredited. All systems of political thought, all 'isms' were
widely regarded as suspect. 'Ideological thinking' was held to involve a blinkered, dogmatic approach. Political opponents were
stigmatised as 'ideological'. Both individual politicians and political
parties were at pains to deny that they were themselves ideological.
Pragmatism was elevated into principle.

This was accompanied by a new optimism that some of the most
important problems in society could be solved, or at least substantially alleviated, by the application of the appropriate techniques. It
was widely reckoned that Keynes had found the answer to mass
unemployment. The new tools of demand management seemed
to promise that never again should millions be made unwillingly
idle. The deliberate pursuit of economic growth also suggested that
society could look forward to a steady increase in living standards,

1

which would effectively eliminate poverty and materially reduce inequality. New breeds of professional technocrats confidently advocated and applied solutions to a variety of social problems.

The 'end of ideology' was perceived as a world, or at least western world, phenomenon, but it seemed particularly applicable to Britain. In Britain the new policy solutions were embraced by all major political parties, and all mainstream politicians. Partisan rhetoric was, of course, still employed, but in practice there did not seem to be much difference between Socialist and Conservative approaches to education, health, housing, town planning, industrial relations, and most of all the management of the economy.

This was widely recognised at the time. Crossman (1981, p. 30) quotes Boothby on the new Conservative ministerial appointments in 1951: 'Rab Butler Chancellor! Why, that's Gaitskell all over again, but from Cambridge.' This proved a prophetic observation. The term 'Butskellism' was soon employed to describe the essential similarity of the economic policies pursued by the two chancellors, and later to characterise a whole era of 'consensus politics'.

Socialism and conservatism, once seen as starkly opposed alternatives, increasingly appeared to blend into each other. At one level it might be suggested that socialism had been absorbed into the political culture and system. Macmillan had once provocatively declared that conservatism had always been a paternal form of socialism, and there were, indeed, right-wing critics who suggested that the post-war Conservative governments were heavily infected with the socialist virus. As for the Labour Party, revisionists argued that socialism must adapt to changed circumstances. Nationalisation was now irrelevant. Socialists should pursue greater equality by distributing the benefits of economic growth through a progressive tax system and social welfare. Their critics could see little difference between this revised socialism and 'one nation' conservatism. There appeared to be one orthodox view of the world which had assimilated some Socialist and some progressive Conservative values.

The conventional psephological wisdom suggested a successful electoral strategy required capture of the middle ground. Political parties were perceived as vote-getting machines. Parties competed for votes in much the same way as firms competed for business. In this context, political ideologies were perceived as awkward electoral baggage, better jettisoned. Parties, like firms, should study the market to find out what the punters wanted, and endeavour to supply it. Economic analysis suggested that, in a two-party system, vote maximisation would necessitate both parties adopting similar centrist positions on the political spectrum (Downs, 1957). This analysis seemed to be confirmed by the experience of two-party politics in both the United States and the United Kingdom. Robert McKenzie's (1963) massive study of political parties in Britain suggested that major apparent differences in organisations and principles masked a substantial convergence of practice.

Such an analysis attributes a rather passive role to the electorate. However, many observers saw the political consensus extending beyond Parliament and parties to the nation as a whole. British political culture was considered to exhibit the characteristics of homogeneity, deference and consensus (Punnett, 1987, ch. 1). Class differences were perceived as declining, while other differences were generally regarded as insignificant (Jennings, 1966). Partly this was attributed to growing prosperity. The inter-war recession and its associated miseries had created a fertile political climate for the growth of extremist political ideologies, although even then in Britain communism and fascism had not advanced beyond the political fringe (see Chapter 6). In the post-war era of full employment, welfare provision and rising living standards, radical proposals posed more of a threat than a promise. The language of class politics seemed singularly inappropriate in a 'property-owning democracy' in which an increasing proportion of the old working class were buying their own homes, running their own cars, and enjoying foreign holidays. The phenomenon of 'embourgeoisement' was seen as particularly threatening to the electoral prospects of Labour (Abrams et al., 1960) and the party was urged to shed its old 'cloth cap' image and acquire a more modern, classless approach. In fact, this was already happening at constituency level, where middle-class intellectuals were increasingly displacing manual workers as the leading local party activists (Hindess, 1971).

For some observers this apparent growing social consensus mirrored fundamental changes in the economy and society. Britain was no longer a capitalist society in the old sense of the term; thus, the social divisions associated with nineteenth-century industrial capitalism were outmoded. Ownership of capital was more widely diffused, and besides the important decision-takers were now technocratic managers rather than owners. Control had been effectively divorced from ownership and, in any case, was increasingly subject to influence from a democratically elected government committed to national economic objectives. There was a sizeable and growing public sector, including nationalised industries, which provided substantial leverage over the economy as a whole. The economy was now more properly 'mixed' than 'capitalist' and ideological thinking based on old social and economic cleavages was becoming increasingly irrelevant (Crosland, 1956).

The political consensus on this analysis represented more than mere pragmatic electoral considerations. It reflected an altered economic and social reality where fundamental conflicts of interest had been eradicated. Political ideologies which substantially reflected interests based on these now outmoded divisions, such as old-fashioned socialism, or for that matter *laissez-faire* liberalism, seemed doomed to extinction.

The neglect of political ideas

So, for all kinds of reasons, political ideologies seemed to have a sharply diminished significance in post-war Britain. They were perceived as highly suspect, involving a dogmatic adherence to outmoded convictions, and the antithesis of a modern, pragmatic approach to politics. They were certainly not regarded as a respectable field for academic study. The study of modern politics was increasingly devoted to means rather than ends, political behaviour rather than political ideas.

This was indeed taken to be the very essence of a scientific approach. All social science had been influenced heavily by the logical positivists. Metaphysical speculation was out. Dispassionate examination of social phenomena was in. For the study of politics this involved a greater emphasis on what was quantifiable, such as elections and voting. Of course, more careful regard for evidence and improved statistical analysis provided a valuable corrective to some of the intuitive assumptions and unsubstantiated generalisations which had been current in earlier political studies. But the emphasis on the more easily quantifiable sometimes involved a relative neglect of some aspects of the study of politics.

Ideas were, in one sense, not neglected. On the contrary, systematic opinion polling produced a wealth of data, not previously available, on the ideas of ordinary people on a whole range of issues. This kind of data was heavily drawn upon in work on voting and on more ambitious efforts to describe and compare political cultures (Almond and Verba, 1963). In the study of political parties there has been detailed analysis of, for example, motions submitted by constituency parties to the annual party conference, which provides important insights into the nature and character of grassroots party activism. However, although such expressions of opinion were carefully categorised, measured and analysed, the actual substance of the opinions was not generally considered a proper subject for political science.

Traditional political theory remained until recently a substantial but rather specialised area of study, essentially antiquarian in its approach, devoted to the detailed exegesis of the great texts of Hobbes, Locke, Bentham and Mill. The implication was that the study of political ideas was scarcely relevant to the modern world. The study of political theory at institutions of higher education, where it was still carried out, generally stopped short in the nineteenth century with Mill and possibly Marx. Twentieth-century political thinkers and twentieth-century political ideas were not considered subjects worthy of academic study.

The rebirth of ideology

It is now clear that the announcement of the end of political ideology was at least premature. Ideas are back in fashion. From the late 1960s or early 1970s the post-war political consensus was fractured, and replaced by ideological polarisation as far as the two major British political parties were concerned (Plant, in Drucker *et al.*, 1983). Variants of Marxism and classical liberalism, ideologies widely regarded as outmoded and irrelevant in the era of consensus politics, showed renewed vitality. This was accompanied by a proliferation of new (or at least newly recognised) perspectives outside the former two-party consensus. A revived nationalist fervour in Scotland and Wales, an essentially new breed of feminism, the increased relevance of ethnic divisions in politics, and the environmental movement had all helped to produce a far more diverse political scene where a wide variety of ideas were contending for · attention.

None of this could have happened had not the old political consensus been broken. It was never, of course, as monolithic as some conventional analysis suggested (including that above in the first section of this chapter). There were always some important differences even between the front benches in Parliament, and certainly there were significant dissenting elements who opposed the prevailing orthodoxy in both major parties. And right through the 1950s and 1960s there were individual thinkers who continued to peddle then deeply unfashionable views – thinkers who, in some cases, have since been hailed as major prophets.

Yet it may still be argued that the consensus was no myth, largely, perhaps, because the prevailing orthodoxy actually seemed to work. In one sense the consensus broke down because the orthodox prescriptions stopped working. The optimism that the major social and economic problems were solved or at least were soluble was displaced by hard evidence to the contrary. The rediscovery of poverty, increased public awareness of homelessness, the apparent failure of much previous housing and planning policy, the growth of family breakdown with accompanying social problems, evidence of growing social unrest culminating in riots in major cities, these all helped to dissolve comfortable assumptions of a society which was good and bound to get better.

Recognition of these problems, although clearly significant and chastening, did not immediately involve the destruction of the political consensus, however. It was possible to argue that they were all in principle soluble, given adequate public funds and appropriate new policies. A plethora of reports produced analysis and recommendations which commanded widespread assent across the political spectrum.

Much more significant was the apparent breakdown of the assumptions on which the whole post-war economic order rested. The simultaneous growth of inflation and unemployment in the 1970s should have been impossible, according to conventional Keynesian analysis. Keynesian remedies were accordingly also discredited. A Labour prime minister sadly asserted that spending your way out of a recession was no longer an option. Crosland, the arch revisionist of the 1950s, who had then declared that the country stood on the edge of mass abundance, now bluntly announced that the party was over.

All this had, of course, considerable implications for the new (or at least newly discovered) social problems identified above. Previously, there had been a general assumption that economic growth, fuelled by Keynesian demand management, would provide the additional resources necessary for social reform. Keynes had helped to make public expenditure respectable, in certain circumstances at least. But the apparent failure of Keynesianism involved a throwback to an earlier era when public expenditure had always been regarded as inherently suspect. Higher public spending was seen as incompatible with a healthy, growing economy. Policy prescriptions for social problems which required higher public spending were increasingly seen as unrealistic in some quarters, and prompted a search for radically different solutions which did not involve 'throwing (government or taxpayers') money' at them. Thus, the previous consensus which had substantially existed on a whole range of issues – child poverty, care of the disabled, homelessness, inner-city policy – was dissolved. Analysis and prescription increasingly reflected fundamentally divergent assumptions.

For if Keynesian economic science was found to be deeply flawed, the search was on for new paradigms. Not surprisingly, this involved a re-emergence of the ideologies which Keynesianism had apparently displaced, socialism and old-style liberalism. In both major parties there were those who sought a return to fundamentals. For many Socialists, if Keynesian style economic planning could not deliver full employment, social reform, and significant progress towards greater equality, then the case was made for a return to common ownership and socialist planning. Equally, for many Conservatives, if Keynesian analysis and prescriptions, coupled with a moderate consensus approach on industrial relations and social issues generally, could not deliver economic growth, a degree of social harmony, and electoral success, the gut reaction was to turn back to free market values.

On the left there were, of course, always Marxists and others who argued that what was represented in the 1950s and 1960s as the end of ideology involved instead the general acceptance of one dominant ideology. The new post-war Keynesian orthodoxy, it was pointed out, rested on certain assumptions about society and human nature. Keynes was supporting an essentially capitalist economy and society, where the ownership of productive wealth remained heavily concentrated. Substantial inequalities were implicitly endorsed. Moreover, the so-called 'mixed economy' of the post-war years remained in most important respects a capitalist economy. Keynesian planning involved a degree of government manipulation of economic aggregates at the macroeconomic level, leaving market forces to operate at the level of individual enterprises and whole industries. Economic science thus served to legitimate a distribution of income and wealth which remained profoundly unequal.

The left also questioned pluralist assumptions about the nature and distribution of political power, and suggested that much which passed for value-free political science was actually highly ideological. Power and influence was not widely dispersed, as liberal pluralists suggested, but concentrated. The whole economic and social system served to reinforce the values of capitalism, free markets and private enterprise. While conventional economic and political theory suggested that individuals were the best judge of their own interests, radicals suggested that this was not necessarily so. Real choices were not presented, but even if they were, the effective conditioning of the people through education, the mass media and the whole socialisation process would ensure the rejection of radical alternatives to the status quo.

Neo-liberals started from quite different assumptions. For them it was axiomatic that the expressed interests of individuals were their real interests. Individuals naturally pursued their own self-interest, and were the best judge of that interest. Socialist suggestions to the contrary implied paternalism, condescension, and bureaucratic interference, summed up in the saying 'the man in Whitehall knows best'. Neo-liberals sought to return power to individuals, with the implicit assumption that individuals did have real economic power (through the market) and, perhaps to a lesser extent, political power (through the ballot box). Collective provision was always suspect, as it involved imposing preferences, interfering with individual freedom and distorting market choice.

To neo-liberals the era of consensus politics had not shored up private enterprise and the capitalist system, as Marxist critics alleged, but had fundamentally undermined it. Keynesian economics had legitimised a massive growth in public spending which had stimulated inflation and harmed the economy. The vested interests of public service employees and recipients of benefits provided powerful pressures for an ever-expanding public sector. Electoral competition forced the parties to respond to the demands of these and other interests in a public auction of promises. Both parties also sought to buy off labour unrest and wider social unrest by making expensive concessions in terms of pay, benefits, and participation in policy making. Such policies had undermined incentives and destroyed the natural discipline of the labour market. High welfare spending could not solve social problems. On the contrary it sapped individual initiative, and created additional social problems. Keynesianism was far from being a neutral technocratic tool of economic management. It involved, rather, creeping socialism.

Thus, Marxists and neo-liberals provided strongly contrasting critical analyses of the assumptions behind the formerly prevailing ideological consensus. Yet it would be simplistic to suggest that consensus was replaced by an ideological polarisation between Marxist socialism on the one hand and classical liberalism on the other. On the right there were (and remain) significant neo-conservative as well as neo-liberal elements in the general critique of consensus politics, and there were (and remain) considerable differences of emphasis among free market advocates. On the left there were, as always, sharply conflicting tendencies.

Nor, of course, was the rejection of Keynesian economics and consensus politics anything like universal. Some Keynesians suggested that there was nothing essentially wrong with the traditional Keynesian remedies. Others suggested that Keynes had been vulgarised and misinterpreted, and that his real message was as valid as ever. Still others suggested that an inadequate political and administrative system had failed to apply a Keynesian approach properly (Hutton, 1986), an analysis which chimed in with a growing critique of British political institutions. This assumed that a national political consensus still substantially existed. Ideological polarisation at Westminster was the artificial product of an outdated electoral system and adversarial procedures in Parliament (Finer, 1975). Many who shared these views coalesced around a revived political centre.

Cutting across these contending schools of thought were, increasingly, political perspectives which reflected differences based on nation, ethnicity, and gender, and an essentially new green ideology. Some of these developments will be explored in more detail later. For the moment, it is sufficient to observe that a political scene which had plausibly appeared to involve the end of ideology, or, rather, the general acceptance of a dominant ideology, has been replaced by one which involves a maelstrom of competing ideas and perspectives. Much policy analysis and prescription is no longer accepted as a neutral technical exercise, but is recognised as the reflection of ideological assumptions which can be challenged from a different perspective. Political ideologies are thus no longer seen as outdated and irrelevant, but rather as essential for an understanding of the mainsprings of political behaviour and public policy.

There has in fact been a considerable revival in academic interest in political ideas, including traditional political theory, political philosophy, and the study of modern political ideologies. These are, of course, overlapping fields of study, but each implies a rather distinctive approach. It is with political ideologies that this work is essentially concerned, and so it is necessary to proceed to some further exploration of what has hitherto been taken for granted – the nature of political ideologies.

What is ideology?

At the beginning of this chapter it was suggested that ideology often has a pejorative connotation, associated with blinkered dogmatism, extremism and illusion (McLennan, 1986, p. 1). It is also a highly contested concept. Many key words used in political, philosophical and social science discourse are unfortunately used in widely different senses, and the term 'ideology' has been defined and employed in extremely varied and even contradictory ways. One recent account identified some twenty-seven distinctive 'definitional elements' drawn from the mass of literature on the subject (Hamilton, 1987).

Here, the concept of ideology will be taken to mean any more or less coherent system of beliefs or views on politics and society. This is the more inclusive, neutral definition of the term, derived from writers as diverse as Gramsci and Mannheim, which is now fairly generally used, at least in academic writing on ideology (Seliger, 1976, p. 14; Greenleaf, 1983, Vol. II, p. 7; Evans, 1984, p. 131; Hamilton, 1987, p. 38). Yet it has to be admitted that the more pejorative and restricted use of the term has a long history, both among Marxists and non-Marxists (McLennan, 1986).

It is impossible to ignore Marx (1818–83) and his successors on the subject of ideology, not only becaue the concept is central to

Marxist thought, but because so many of the issues they have raised are still live. Crucially, there is the question of the relationship of political ideas to material interests and questions of power and domination on the one hand and science and truth on the other. Are political ideologies ultimately just rationalisations of self-interest? Do they simply reflect the interests of dominant groups? Is it impossible to adjudge between the rival claims of ideologies, or are some 'true' and others 'false', some scientifically-based and others unscientific?

Marx was concerned with the source of ideas. One of his targets was idealism, the philosophical approach, derived ultimately from Plato but featuring especially Kant (1724–1804) and Hegel (1770–1831), which suggested that ideas are the ultimate reality and the motive force in human history. Against this, Marx presented his own materialist conception of history in which ideas derive from the material circumstances of humanity. 'Life is not determined by consciousness, but consciousness by life'. (Marx, 1977, p. 164)

Ideas reflect social and economic circumstances. Marx, moreover, saw society as deeply divided, so that the moral and political ideas expressed at any time reflect ultimately conflicting class interests. But the prevailing ideas, Marx suggested, will reflect the existing power structure, the current pattern of domination and subordination, partly because those with economic and political power will be well placed to control the dissemination and legitimation of ideas, through, for example, education and the mass media. Thus, 'the ideas of the ruling class are in every epoch the ruling ideas'. (Marx, 1977, p. 176)

It follows that subordinate classes will not necessarily recognise the real basis of society, not their own exploitation, but will hold a distorted, mistaken view of reality. Marx commonly used the term 'ideology' to describe this distorted view that a social class, such as the industrial proletariat, might have of its own position in society as a whole. Much of the prevailing wisdom of his day, such as the ideas of the classical economists, Smith, Malthus and Ricardo, Marx regarded as ideological rather than scientific. Their theories served the interests of capitalism. By contrast, Marx thought his own method provided a powerful tool for penetrating below the surface and understanding the real economic and social forces which shape change. In this sense, Marxism was science rather than ideology.

This identification of ideology with illusion and distortion and what Engels later called 'false consciousness' (McLennan, 1986, p. 18) is, of course, highly pejorative. However, Marx sometimes used it in a more neutral sense, and this is the sense in which later Marxists, such as Lenin, Gramsci and Lukacs, have developed the discussion of ideology. The need to counter the dominant ruling-class ideology with a proletarian or socialist ideology was assumed. The latter naturally could not be identified with illusion or false consciousness. The use of the term 'ideology', then, implied nothing as to the truth or falsehood of its content.

Yet this later non-pejorative use of the term by Marxists remains restricted, because ideology is still tied to class interests. Relating political ideas to material interests is certainly a fruitful approach. It does make sense to ask who is putting forward particular doctrines and why, and whose interests they serve. Frequently, the answers will be suggestive, although, of course, the establishment of an interest does not necessarily disprove a theory. Moreover, it is not that difficult to relate major political ideologies with class interests. Thus conservatism, historically, was associated with the landed interest, liberalism with financial and industrial capital, and socialism with the industrial working class.

Non-Marxists would generally reject the close association of ideologies with class interest. Conservatives or liberals would argue that their ideas have a universal relevance, and are to the general benefit of all classes, in so far as they are prepared to recognise class distinctions at all. But one does not have to accept these claims un-critically to ask whether political ideologies always and essentially have to articulate class interests, for where does that leave perspectives which reflect other divisions in society, such as those based on religion, ethnicity or gender?

In practice, Marxists have tended to regard such divisions as either artificially fostered to weaken working-class unity (e.g. nationalism and religion) or derived ultimately from more fundamental class divisions (e.g. race and gender). But of course, there are those for whom issues of race, gender, religion or nationhood are quite fundamental rather than secondary, so that these issues inform their whole perspective on politics, power, decision-making and public policy. In this way, feminism or nationalism may be regarded just as much as political ideologies as those which more plausibly relate to class divisions, such as socialism or liberalism. Yet feminism, nationalism or racism can still be associated with material interests, if not the economic class interests of classical Marxist theory. The Greens arguably present a greater difficulty for Marxists, as their ideology is not ostensibly related to the interest of any specific group within existing human society, but to generations yet unborn, to other species, and to the universe as a whole. While it is possible to relate Green ideas to social interests, this may not be the most useful approach to understanding the ideology.

Modern, particularly American, social scientists have also, like Marx, employed the term ideology in a highly pejorative and restricted manner, but in a quite opposite sense to his. Non-Marxist economists, sociologists and political scientists emphasised the need for detached, value-free, rigorous empirical research – which they saw as the essence of the social science method. Marxist analysis was regarded, by contrast, as dogmatic, unscientific and 'ideological'. Ideology was identified with a blinkered adherence to a system of thought without regard to evidence. Communism and fascism were ideologies, while the liberal pluralist ideas on which post-war western society rested, were scientific and non-ideological.

Both Marxists and non-Marxists, then, have tended to define ideology in a restricted sense, but they have reached diametrically opposed conclusions over which political perspectives should be regarded as ideological. Marx saw ideology as a rationalisation of the status quo, as a self-interested justification of the existing distribution of wealth and power. Many non-Marxists have regarded the status quo in the west as unideological, and the post-war consensus was taken as marking the 'end of ideology'. Revolutionary creeds that threatened consensus, like communism, were ideologies. Marx most of the time (but by no means all Marxists) and Marx's most virulent modern critics have also both used the term in a highly pejorative way. Thus, an ideology is someone else's perspective. To describe a position as 'ideological' is to condemn it.

Such an interpretation of ideology is ultimately rather sterile. Partly for that reason, there is an increasing academic consensus that the term is more usefully employed in an inclusive and neutral, non-pejorative way. Here, ideology will be taken to mean 'any system of ideas and norms directing political and social action' (Flew, 1979, p. 150). The use of the term 'ideology' does not, therefore, by itself imply any kind of judgement on the validity or otherwise of the ideas discussed. Ideology is not to be contrasted with science. Moreover, ideologies are not to be identified exclusively with either the preservation or the overthrow of the status quo. Ideologies may be conservative, reformist or revolutionary. They may be 'moderate' or 'extremist'. Further, although ideologies are often associated with conflict, a system of beliefs which commands general or even universal assent within society may still be characterised as an ideology. The era of consensus politics did not involve the end of ideology, simply the widespread dominance of a single ideology, a situation which for some writers, such as Gramsci, might constitute the norm rather than the exception.

An ideology implies a connected set of beliefs, a whole perspective on the world, rather than a single political principle. Yet it may involve inconsistencies and even contradictions. Moreover, ideologies can be held at a variety of levels. They may be systematically articulated, through, for example, the writings of major thinkers, or expressed more selectively and persuasively through political pamphlets or speeches, or they may be essentially latent and unsophisticated, expressed if at all in shorthand slogans and symbols. Hayek's *Road to Serfdom* (Hayek, 1976), the advertising slogans of Saatchi and Saatchi, the speeches of Margaret Thatcher, the Union Jack, and the headlines in the *Sun* newspaper are all aspects of modern Conservative ideology.

Finally, no definite position is taken here on the vexed question of the relationship between ideology and interest. This may seem craven, or worse, depriving the study of a coherent theoretical framework for analysis (some may feel); but a degree of agnosticism does have the merit of not closing down in advance what might prove to be fruitful areas of study. An idealist position might preclude any investigation of the social background, interests and motivations of those holding particular views. A thoroughgoing materialism would not allow any discussion of the elements of mainstream ideologies in terms which their adherents would allow or understand. Furthermore, it might on *a priori* grounds dismiss all major British ideologies as rationalisations for capitalism with various shades of emphasis. This may be a quite tenable position, but it does rather undermine the case for any extensive examination of ideologies.

In the developing literature, there is work on political ideologies within both the materialist and idealist traditions. A good example of a sophisticated Marxist approach is Stuart Hall's 'Variants of liberalism' (Donald and Hall, 1986) which suggests a subtle interaction between changing class forces and the evolution of liberal ideas that is never crudely reductionist. By contrast, Robert Pearson and Geraint Williams (1984) treat ideologies in an essentially idealist way. Their procedure is to expound first the ideas and principles of particular political ideologies, such as liberalism, conservatism and socialism, and then explore how these ideas were applied in the form of public policy. Their work fits within a political thought tradition which tends to assume that ideas are worth studying in themselves, and is less concerned with where they have come from.

Constituents of ideologies

A broad and somewhat loose definition of ideology rather precludes any categorical assumptions over what an ideology should or should not contain. It may confidently be asserted that all political ideologies contain, implicitly or explicitly, descriptive and prescriptive elements. The prescriptive elements may normally predominate, but any prescription for social action must ultimately rest on some assumptions, however crude, about the nature of existing society and human behaviour. There is thus a picture of the world as it is, which may be more or less accurate or highly distorted, and there is a picture of the world as it should be, which may approximate to what is perceived as the existing picture, or be far removed from it. There is usually some conception also, rudimentary or highly developed, of how the ends which are desired are to be achieved.

Three elements may be broadly identified an interpretation of existing social arrangement, a vision of the future, and a strategy for realising that future. Of course, for those who are broadly happy with existing social arrangements, the vision of the future may closely resemble the present, and the strategy will be one of seeking to maintain the status quo. Those profoundly dissatisfied with the present will contemplate strategies for achieving some kind of revolution.

A view of existing social arrangements will commonly include some assumptions about human nature and individual motivation, and indeed, such assumptions can be seen to lie behind both the ideas of most of the great political thinkers of the past, and, perhaps more implicitly, behind modern political ideologies. It is not difficult to divide political theorists into optimists and pessimists on the subject of human nature. Plato, Machiavelli, and Hobbes, for example, were all fairly pessimistic about the capacity of human beings to live together sociably and co-operatively, without a considerable element of coercion or brainwashing, while Aristotle, Rousseau,. and, in the last analysis, Marx, had a more optimistic view of human potential for fruitful co-operation.

Among modern political ideologies, fascism makes some fairly cynical assumptions about the pliability of man, while anarchism involves what some might consider hugely optimistic assumptions about human nature. Of mainstream ideologies, socialism is essentially optimistic, and traditional conservatism rather pessimistic, about human nature. Between these two concepts, old-style liberalism, drawing heavily on classical economics, sees individuals motivated by self-interest, but suggests that the net consequence of all pursuing their self-interest will be the greatest common good.

A linked consideration is the potential for changing human nature, from which a further question naturally arises. Is human nature the same everywhere, or is it substantially the product of the environment? Does vicious behaviour reflect the immutable nature of humanity, or is it the product of a particular environment, which might be changed? Anarchists for example believe that power corrupts, and a society without hierarchies of authority and without government, in the sense of coercive power, would lead to more co-operative and civilised human behaviour. Socialists tend to think that highly self-interested competitive behaviour is the product of the capitalist economic system rather than a universal human characteristic. They also suggest that substantial inequalities in human capacities and attainments are not innate, but can be reduced through enlarging opportunities. Conservatives are usually rather more sceptical about the scope for improvements in human nature, although they may consider religious belief, or stable family background, possible ameliorative factors. Some feminists would draw a major distinction between male and female human nature, suggesting that men are naturally aggressive and competitive, while women are naturally caring and co-operative, although other feminists would suggest that this behaviour is largely culturally determined and that men could learn to be caring. The capacity for changing human behaviour is clearly important to some ideologies, to the extent that prescriptions for the future may require people to behave in different ways.

This inevitably raises the question of the relationship of the individual to society. Most of the ancient Greeks, including both Plato and Aristotle, saw man as a naturally social and political animal. Aristotle considered that the man outside political society was either a beast or a god, sub-human or superhuman. A proper human existence was not conceivable outside society. At the opposite extreme, liberalism has often tended to see society as an artificial construct, requiring a conscious and deliberate effort to bring it into being, and having no meaning apart from its constituent individual elements. Mrs Thatcher lies comfortably within this liberal political tradition in her assertion that there is no such thing as society, only individuals and their families. By contrast, both traditional conservatism (or Toryism) and socialism have tended to view the individual as inseparable from society, with individuals, groups and whole classes bound inextricably to each other through ties of mutual dependence, although, of course, conservatives would tend to see these unequal relationships in essentially benign terms, while socialists would interpret them in terms of exploitation, at least within existing capitalist society. Finally, in this connection it may be observed that what have been described as totalitarian ideologies involve, in theory at least, the total subjugation of the individual to the national whole.

Ideologies will commonly involve all kinds of other assumptions about the way society currently operates – the extent of equality within society, the organisation of work and industrial relations, community relations, authority and power structures, and a host of further issues. Some of these assumptions may be substantially accurate, while others may be wildly inaccurate, but perceptions of how the world is inevitably colour perceptions of how it should be, so that description and prescription are closely interlinked. In the 1970s, for example, it was widely believed that trade unions ran the country, and that Mr Jack Jones, then general secretary of the Transport and General Workers' Union, was more powerful than the prime minister – purportedly a description of the then existing state of affairs. Not surprisingly perhaps, in view of this widespread conviction, many people also thought that trade unions were too powerful (an evaluation) and that their power should be reduced (a prescription).

Prescriptions for the future are therefore bound to depend on perceptions of present arrangements and attitudes towards them. Some people may be more fearful than desirous of change – for all sorts of reasons. They may be substantial beneficiaries of existing social arrangements. They may pessimistically fear that change is likely to be for the worse. They may be persuaded, perhaps against what others would regard as their objective interests, that change is impossible, dangerous, or undesirable. The essence of conservatism, as the term implies, is to avoid major change, and a radically different future is neither sought nor desired, although a degree of gradual reform may be countenanced. Some reactionaries, in the proper sense of the term, may seek a future which resembles a past, real or imaginary, which they regret. Others may strive for a future which is nothing like the present or immediate past. The construction of utopias has been a favourite pastime of political thinkers since classical times.

The problem with utopias is how to achieve them. The proposed utopia may be far more appealing than existing society, but how does one progress from (a) to (b)? Ideologies generally involve some assumptions about social change, although this element can in practice be fairly weak. Marx was critical of some of his socialist predecessors for lacking any coherent theory of social change. They had a socialist vision of the future, but no realistic strategy for achieving that socialist vision. A major debate among socialists since Marx's day has been over the prospects of the parliamentary road to socialism – whether socialism can be achieved solely or mainly through the ballot box and the election of governments with parliamentary majorities. Some socialists deny that this is possible. Parliamentary socialists tend to respond that the alternatives are even more problematic.

For conservatives the problem is rather how to maintain social stability, and avoid social unrest and revolution. The choice may often seem to lie between granting reforms to appease dissatisfied elements, or refusing any concessions for fear that these will only fuel demands for further change and create more instability in the long run. In general, conservatives are much more sceptical of the scope for deliberate social engineering than liberals or socialists, and more wary of the possible dangers of change.

Levels of ideology

Political ideologies may be expressed at a number of different levels, from the relatively sophisticated to the crude or even latent.

Some great thinkers studied within the political theory tradition have clearly made a significant contribution to particular political ideologies – Marx to socialism, and, perhaps, Burke to conservatism or Bentham to liberalism. But there are writers who have attracted particular attention from other political thinkers or from modern academics who have had relatively little obvious impact on subsequent political movements – Hobbes, for example, generally rated as the most important political thinker that Britain has produced. It may, of course, be true that many of Hobbes's ideas have generally permeated the British political tradition, but it is difficult to identify him positively with a particular ideology.

Often, writers who would not be categorised as major political thinkers have had wider influence, and perhaps contributed more towards the development and acceptance of particular ideologies. Harriet Martineau, who wrote little fables embodying the principles of classical economics, Edward Baines, the polemical editor of the *Leeds Mercury*, and Samuel Smiles, the purveyor of Victorian homilies on self-help and other virtues were more widely read and understood than Ricardo or Nassau Senior, and in some ways can be considered more typical of *laissez-faire* liberalism.

At another level, the pronouncements and achievements of active politicians, which would not command space or attention in histories of political theory, may play a critical role in the development of ideologies and be important for their subsequent interpretation. There are very few great texts which provide much of a guide to an understanding of conservatism. Many interpretations place particular emphasis on the contribution of past politicians, especially prime ministers, such as Peel, Disraeli, Salisbury, or Baldwin to the development of conservatism. Some of these politicians did articulate their ideas with varying degrees of sophistication in articles, novels, or carefully constructed speeches and manifestos, but the ideas of others must be substantially derived from their behaviour and output in office. For while political ideologies, almost by definition, influence political behaviour, they can also sometimes appear as *post hoc* rationalisations of political behaviour, although few politicians would put it quite as bluntly as Herbert Morrison, who declared that socialism was what the Labour government did.

Ideologies are not just the possession of the political classes, however. They are held by the masses, and although there may be a difference in sophistication between the elite and mass versions of particular ideologies, they normally recognisably belong to the same kind of outlook on life, and interrelate. Mrs Thatcher acknowledges the influence of the everyday maxims acquired during her upbringing in that celebrated grocer's shop in Grantham (Young, 1989, p. 5) but also acknowledges a debt to Adam Smith and Hayek (Thatcher, 1977), and it is difficult to assess which has made the more significant contribution to what has come to be termed 'Thatcherism'.

It can be confidently asserted that it is the everyday maxims which have a greater resonance with the wider public. Newspaper headlines, slogans and graffiti, and non-verbal symbols, such as the British bulldog, or Britannia, or photographic images, may reinforce or express particular ideological approaches. Some political ideologies are indeed almost entirely lacking in sophisticated intellectual expression. The Nuremberg rallies and the slogans painted in Mussolini's Italy, 'Believe, Obey, Fight', 'Live dangerously', 'Better one day as a lion than a thousand years as a sheep', perhaps tell us more about the nature of fascism, and certainly had more influence on political behaviour, than the generally rather thin fascist literature.

Ideologies then can be interpreted and analysed at a number of different levels – from sophisticated intellectual constructs down to inferences from political behaviour. The clenched fist may seem a long way removed from Marx's *Das Kapital* but they are both aspects of one ideology. The different levels are also intricately interrelated. It should be re-emphasised, however, that the non-rational or irrational ways in which ideologies are sometimes made manifest does not necessarily invalidate their interpretation of the world or their message. To take an obvious analogy, it would not generally be regarded as fair to judge the truth of some of the world's major religions from the sometimes crude utterances and bizarre practices of their less-educated adherents. On the other hand, such behaviour may tell us as much about a particular religion as the sacred texts associated with it. Both require investigation for a full picture.

Power, influence and indoctrination

Consideration of the ideological perspectives of the masses raises some awkward questions on the transmission of ideas – over, for example, the potential for deliberate indoctrination. There are some celebrated fictional accounts of thought control, and plenty of real life illustrations of more or less successful attempts to mould opinion, by no means all of which are to be found in so-called totalitarian states. For example, the allied authorities in Germany after the war embarked on a deliberate counter-indoctrination programme which employed many of the means of their Nazi predecessors – censorship of newspapers, burning of books, screening teachers for ideological soundness, and the like.

Most attempts to influence people's minds on political issues are less extensive and systematic than this, but there is still a certain amount of quite conscious manipulation, even in a supposed liberal democracy like Britain. Television commercials have been extensively and expensively employed to promote the activities of 'your local electricity business' and 'your local water business'. Quite apart from other questions raised by these commercials, the use of the term 'business' is clearly deliberate and significant. Although the term can be employed by academics in a broader sense, its popular association is with the private sector, and it has decidedly different associations from the word 'authority' or 'board' which were previously used. It both prepares the public for the privatisation of these industries, and promotes the values and ideas associated with the private sector and commerical enterprise.

If deliberate manipulation of people's minds by the government or the dominant element in society was regularly employed and always successful, there would be no ideological conflict, just the universal acceptance of one ideology. Plato wanted to eliminate conflict in this way in his ideal state, and there have been celebrated recent fictional examples, such as Orwell's *1984* and Huxley's *Brave New World*. Real live governments have found it rather more difficult to stifle all dissent.

The role of the media in shaping opinion is another controversial area. The liberal pluralist assumption was that people were exposed to a wide range of sources and views, enabling them to make up their own mind on political questions. Academic research in the 1960s suggested that people used the media to reinforce their own ideas, and tended to filter out information which did not match their preconceived attitudes. This implied that the media influence on attitudes was relatively slight. At that time, also, there was a rough balance in the partisan leanings of the national press, and any newspaper bias was assumed to be modified by a strictly non-partisan television.

These comforting conclusions have been somewhat undermined of late. The narrow concentration of ownership and control of the media has re-awakened fears of the power of the press (Newton, in Drucker *et al.*, 1986). There is now a clear party bias in the national press, and mass circulation tabloids exhibit extensive and quite deliberate political propaganda, although this is not realised by all their readers (Seymour-Ure, 1974). The assumption of television neutrality has been challenged by the radical left and some of the right (Glasgow University Media Group, 1976; 1982). Additionally and critically, more recent research is less confident of the capacity of people to resist or filter out the extensive political propaganda to which they are exposed. The views of the masses – the popular expression of political ideologies – may reflect media influence. Dearlove and Saunders (1984, p. 352) conclude: 'It is too crude to suggest that the papers tell us what to think; but they do to a large extent tell us how to think it.'

Too much emphasis should not perhaps be placed on deliberate in-doctrination by governments or media propaganda. Far more significant, it might be argued, is the largely unconscious process by which beliefs are transmitted and sustained from the elite to the masses, and across generations. Existing institutions, work practices, patterns of social organisation, habits and beliefs may generally be taken for granted. In some cases it may require a considerable effort to even imagine alternatives. The weight of tradition is always likely to be a major constraint on political thinking, which will tend to rationalise the status quo and serve the interests of those who benefit principally from it. On the whole, the ideas of established dominant groups will tend to be accepted throughout society, without any deliberation action to ensure this. And while the dominant ideology may not be all pervasive, some of its core assumptions at least may gain wide acceptance among subordinate groups.

Parkin (1972, ch. 3) usefully distinguishes between dominant, subordinate, and radical meaning systems. The dominant value system 'will tend to set the standards for what is considered objectively "right"' throughout society. Parkin points out that these generally accepted standards will affect artistic values and linguistic usages, as well as the more critical rules for the allocation and distribution of resources. The subordinate value system is grounded in the direct experiences of the local working-class community but is 'essentially accommodative', involving adaptation towards, rather than endorsement of, or outright opposition to, dominant values. Parkin instances trade unionism as an example of a subordinate value system. While trade unionism springs directly from working-class experience, and involves attempts by the organised working class to secure better wages and conditions through collective bargaining, it does not normally amount to a fundamental challenge to the existing economic system, but rather can be seen as an accommodation with capitalism. A radical value system involves a clear alternative to the existing social and political order, such as might be presented by a socialist party. Parkin's own analysis suggests how difficult it is to secure mass support for such a radical alternative value system. It seems unlikely to emerge spontaneously from working-class experience, and although Parkin suggests that an organised working-class party may be able to articulate and sustain a mass following for a radical alternative, he also acknowledges how far in practice socialist parties have abandoned radical aims, and sought accommodation with the existing capitalist order.

It is not necessary to follow Parkin's argument in every particular to recognise that there is a clear connection between the distribution of economic and political power on the one hand, and ideological competition on the other. The battle of ideas is inevitably fought with loaded dice. The failure of some political perspectives, such as radical feminism, or anarchism, or dark-green environmentalism, to gain a wider following may reflect inherent weaknesses in the ideology. Alternatively, it may be an indication of the overwhelming difficulties any radical perspective faces in combatting the mass of routinely accepted assumptions bound up with the existing economic and social order. Yet it may not just be radical left-wing views which fail to secure a fair hearing. Both neo-liberals and neo-conservatives have claimed that the post-war progressive Keynesian consensus effectively excluded their ideas from political debate until recently.

Theory and reality – ideology and public policy

It is the constant two-way interplay between ideas and action which is perhaps the essence of political ideologies. Ideologies evolve and develop through experience of reality. Marx's writings may be reinterpreted by every age, but the texts remain the same. Socialism as a political ideology has had to evolve to take into account developments as varied as a universal adult franchise, two world wars, the Russian Revolution, the General Strike, the Great Depression, the Welfare State, Keynesianism and economic growth, decolonisation and the emergence of the third world. Such developments inevitably provoked some reassessment of cherished nostrums – some might argue not enough, and indeed would suggest that conservatism has been more adaptable.

A common consequence has been internal tension and division – between socialism and social democracy, for example, which are now sometimes presented as essentially separate ideologies. There was a similar tension within liberalism around the turn of the century between old-style free market liberalism, and the New Liberalism. In such circumstances the reformers feel that they are extending and updating principles to take account of a changed world, while traditional adherents feel that fundamental principles are being ignored or betrayed. There has been a similar debate among conservatives since the Second World War over the extent to which conservatism should make concessions to the altered circumstances and altered expectations of the post-war world.

But if ideologies are constantly evolving and adapting to changed circumstances, they are also constantly influencing political and social action. Ideological perceptions influence, for example, whether people vote, and how they vote. They will influence how individuals, groups and communities will react to proposed and actual developments which adversely affect them – from passive acquiescence, through various forms of lobbying to civil disobedience and ultimately violence. They will influence the kind of demands which are made of government and how these are pursued. And they will also quite fundamentally affect legislation and other outputs of government.

Public policy quite clearly reflects ideological assumptions, and in turn can influence people's ideological perceptions. The sale of council houses is an obvious illustrative example. The policy may be said to reflect Conservative convictions on the merits of private ownership, and free market values. But the opportunity which many council house tenants took to purchase their own houses, arguably had an impact on their political perceptions, and subsequently their political behaviour, including perhaps their voting behaviour.

The relationship between ideology and public policy has become a fruitful area of study. Laying bare the ideological assumptions behind particular measures provides a useful approach to policy analysis, which avoids the bland consensus interpretations of much social and political history. There is often the implication that particular outcomes were the only possible course of action following the cumulative endeavours of enlightened reformers of all convictions and none, working in the general public interest. Uncovering the ideological assumptions behind particular policies does not, of course, necessarily invalidate them, but does provide a basis for criticism and the analysis of alternatives. Why, for example, did Beveridge consider the insurance principle so important in his social security scheme? He might have recommended that benefits should be financed out of general taxation (as, in effect, they substantially have been). Beveridge's own Liberalism, and the broadly small 'l' liberal assumptions of much of the then political establishment, provide some explanation.

A number of useful studies have explored this relationship between ideology and public policy – for example, Fraser's *Evolution of the Welfare State*, George and Wilding's *Ideology and Social Welfare*, Pearson and Williams's *Political Thought and Public Policy in the Nineteenth Century*, and W. H. Greenleaf's massive *The British Political Tradition*. The implication of this growing and diverse body of work is that public policy cannot be properly understood without an understanding of the political ideologies which infuse them, while ideologies have to be explained in terms of political behaviour and governmental output as well as ideas and principles. This is as good a justification as any for the rest of this book. Far from being dead, as Daniel Bell (1960) asserted, political ideologies are alive and flourishing, and are of critical importance for the study of social science.

2

The British Political Tradition

Why British political ideologies?

Most, if not all, of the ideologies referred to in the opening chapter are essentially international. Moreover the specifically British contribution to these ideologies has not been particularly impressive in intellectual terms. Britain appears almost a backwater in the evolution of socialism, with few thinkers or politicians warranting extended consideration in any general history (e.g. Lichtheim, 1970). Ideologies of the right are less internationalist and more culture specific, yet it might still be suggested that with the partial exception of Burke, Britain has provided no sustained intellectually coherent defence of conservative or reactionary politics to compare with continental or American writing. British conservatism is thus largely empty of explicit theoretical content, and its essence has to be inferred from practice. The British contribution to liberalism is rather more impressive, although the general insularity of British thinking about politics is again evident from the general ignorance in this country of the European liberal tradition. While continental accounts of liberalism pay due tribute to British liberal thinkers, the compliment is rarely returned. Even Arblaster's (1984) stimulating book on western liberalism is somewhat anglocentric. Nor is the British element in more recently developed ideologies any more significant. Green and feminist thinking have been more impressively explored in other countries.

So why *British* political ideologies? It might be objected that any account of ideologies centring on Britain is bound to leave out a great deal of what is important. Not only does it necessarily involve a somewhat intellectually impoverished account of socialism and conservatism, it also virtually omits altogether some ideologies which are important on an international scale, such as anarchism. But, in general, a concentration on British ideologies might be held to reflect and confirm an insularity in the British intellectual tradition which is less than admirable.

However, that very insularity provides a kind of justification. British political ideologies are clearly related to wider ideologies which transcend national boundaries, and as such are obviously susceptible to foreign influences – an account of British socialism which made no reference at all to Marx might reasonably be re-garded as deficient. Yet they are also to a degree *sui generis*, of their own kind. British liberalism, conservatism, and socialism have all developed in a distinctive way. All mainstream British ideologies have been influenced by a British political, economic and social history which has exhibited some markedly different features from experiences elsewhere. There is thus a British political tradition which has left its mark on all our major political ideologies, even those which, like socialism, are ostensibly internationalist in assumptions. And it goes without saying that it is these British variants of political ideologies which influence British political behaviour, and British public policy.

The British political tradition

Any account of the British political tradition is bound to be highly selective, over-simplified, and personal, the more particularly so when it is conceived as a brief prelude to the explanation of modern British political ideologies. It might also be regarded as superfluous and perhaps rather presumptuous in the light of Greenleaf's (1983) massive exploration of the same field; so, perhaps it should first be explained how this brief excursion differs in approach from Green-leaf's and some other recent writers'.

At the risk of aggravating charges of superficiality, this account of the British political tradition goes back considerably earlier, and is somewhat broader in scope. Greenleaf is not really concerned with much before the nineteenth century, and his whole work is conceived in the shape of a dialectical debate between libertarianism and collectivism (Vol. I, pp. 14–28). He is less concerned with the development of specific ideologies, except in relation to this central theme. This account begins considerably earlier because it is suggested that mainstream British political ideologies, and British political culture generally, have been shaped by experience prior to the Industrial Revolution, although it is of course acknowledged that the transformation of the British economy and society through industrialisation quite fundamentally affected British politics. It is also considered that there are other themes worth exploring besides the conflict between libertarianism and collectivism, important though this is.

It might be assumed that an account of the British political tradition would consist of a potted history of British political thought. The choice here has been to centre on the long-term impact of particular historical developments. More specifically this account focuses on the impact on British political thinking of six major historical influences: first, the Reformation and religious upheavals of the sixteenth century; second, the political upheavals of the seventeenth century, third, the establishment of the British Constitution and political stability from the eighteenth century onwards; fourth, the impact of industrialisation over the last two hundred years or so; fifth, the effect of war; and finally, the legacy of empire.

Some reference to the ideas of major political thinkers is made in the context of these historical developments, but their thought is not explored in any systematic way. Partly, this is because there are so many full expositions and also good concise accounts of the major British political thinkers that any recapitulation of their ideas would seem superfluous. But chiefly, it is considered that in the last analysis the experience of civil war, for example, had rather more effect on subsequent political thinking and behaviour in Britain than the writing of Thomas Hobbes. British history itself has shaped British political ideas. This is more obviously the case where the focus, as here, is on the evolution of broad political ideologies which can be examined at a number of levels, from the highly articulate and conscious elaborations of key thinkers and political leaders, to the largely unconscious and implicit assumptions of the masses.

To attempt to demonstrate how British history, has influenced the development of British political ideologies might seem a far more perilous enterprise than a conventional account of British political thought. The past is not 'given'. Contemporaries disagreed about the meaning and significance of the momentous events such as the Reformation or the English Civil War which they lived through, and historians have continued to disagree about them ever since. Key episodes in British history have been repeatedly reinterpreted.

Moreover, while these episodes have clearly had an effect on subsequent thinking about politics, it is equally true that later political ideas have contributed to the reinterpretation of the past. Sometimes a powerful myth has been created with the benefit of hindsight, and from the standpoint of victorious groups and interests, and this in turn has reinforced the dominant ideology. Something of the sort perhaps occurred with the so-called Glorious Revolution of 1688. The interpretation of history is often a critical ingredient in political ideologies, and the winners who have emerged from the struggles of the past have, not surprisingly, sought to rewrite that past to suit their own interests.

Inevitably, then, our understanding of the past is influenced by our understanding of the present, and equally our modern political ideologies involve an interpretation of the past. This is more obvious in some other countries than in Britain. In France, the interpretation and reinterpretation of the last 200 years of French history have been an inseparable element of ideological conflict.

Yet, while any account of the key formative influences on subsequent political thinking is bound to be highly selective and subjective, it is worth attempting, for it is impossible to explain the distinctive development of British political ideologies without reference to the historical context within which they have been shaped.

The impact of the Reformation and the religious upheavals of the sixteenth century

The English Reformation begun by Henry VIII in the sixteenth century may seem a somewhat remote starting point for an exploration of the British political tradition, the more particularly as Britain was then a geographical expression rather than a political reality. Yet it was an event of quite fundamental importance in this country's history, with not only major immediate consequences, but also long-term political implications, some of which have persisted to the present day.

It is a truism that, following the Reformation, England was no longer part of the Roman Catholic family of nations. That alone, however, had major implications for the content and style of its politics. The politics of Catholic countries today have a different flavour from those where Catholics are in a minority. Church–state relations have evolved differently. In some cases the Church has been built into the state, in other cases the state and the Church have been at odds (Italy before Mussolini's Concordat, or France under the Third Republic). Either way, religion has generally continued to play a more significant part in politics. It is sometimes explicitly recognised in the Constitution. It has spawned Catholic political parties, and Catholic trade unions. It has influenced voting, and Church leaders have not on occasion shrunk from giving explicit instructions to their flock over how to exercise their vote. The close involvement of the Church in politics, and sometimes its association with a wealthy establishment, has also often provoked an anticlerical reaction among liberals and socialists. There is thus an anticlerical tradition among French, Spanish and Italian liberals, republicans, radicals and socialists which is largely absent in Britain.

A more problematic, contestable legacy of the English Reformation was the early development of capitalism. It was Weber (1864–1920) who suggested that Protestantism, or more specifically Calvinism, was particularly congenial to the development of values which favoured capitalist accumulation. Tawney (1938) and others have applied Weber's thesis to England, associating Puritanism with the spirit of mercantile and subsequently industrial capitalism. The evidence is suggestive, but inconclusive, yet if there is anything in the theory, then the initially rather arbitrary and accidental removal of England from the Catholic sphere had momentous long-term implications for the country's economic development, and ways of thinking about economics and politics. Samuel Smiles's little Victorian homilies on self-help might be seen as an expression of an essentially Protestant ethic which can be traced back to the Reformation.

While the connection between the Reformation and the rise of capitalism is speculative and contentious, the continuing divisive effect it had, not only on religious conviction and observance but also on society and politics, is almost too obvious to require restatement. Within England the Reformation established religious divisions which have persisted to the present day. Henry VIII of course had no intention of establishing freedom of conscience in religious matters. He had merely substituted himself for the Pope as head of the English Church. He sought to impose a new, only slightly altered, orthodoxy to replace the one he had overthrown. Yet his successors failed to impose a uniform religous system. Catholicism could not be restored, as Mary and later James II discovered, but it also could not be totally suppressed. Nor, it transpired, could the sovereign impose uniformity of religious observance on Protestants.

Scarcely anyone in the sixteenth or early seventeenth centuries championed religious toleration, however. True believers of all persuasions hoped for the triumph of their righteous cause, and the more passionate adherents were prepared to die for it. The divisions in English society which the Reformation caused cut to an extent across class and other divisions. They remained bitter for centuries. Catholics became a persecuted and feared minority – a potential Trojan horse within the nation. Guy Fawkes Day was not in the seventeenth and eighteenth centuries a harmless diversion, but a rather grisly reminder of potential Catholic treachery. Effectively, Catholics remained second-class citizens until the Catholic Emancipation Act in 1829. Puritans also suffered from persecution from the reign of Elizabeth onwards, and the subsequent division between Anglicans and Nonconformists had enduring consequences.

In the late seventeenth century the Tories emerged as the party of the established Church of England, while the Whigs championed the right to dissent and religious toleration. These divisions remained important for the Conservative and Liberal parties in the nineteenth century and through to the early twentieth century. The religious question then inspired far more political controversy, and had a larger impact on party allegiances and voting behaviour than economic issues. While today it is of diminished significance, the legacy of religious differences still affects the ethos and character of modern political parties. For example, the Labour Party inherited something of the Whig/Liberal Nonconformist tradition, and this is one of the factors which explains the distinctive flavour of British socialism.

But the English Reformation did not just sow the seeds of religious divisions with enduring political implications. It virtually established England as a sovereign nation state. Whatever his motives, Henry VIII had effectively asserted England's sovereign independence against the universalist claims of the papacy. This was a symbolic act which both reflected and assisted trends already in progress. The final loss of the Hundred Years War had forced the Tudors to concentrate their attention on the government of England, and allowed the development of an English nation state and an English national culture.

Before the sixteenth century it might be questioned whether there was much of a distinctive English, let alone British, tradition of thought. England was part of a western Christian culture. Latin was the lingua franca of the educated classes, and virtually all serious writing on theology, philosophy and history was in Latin. Also, from the Norman Conquest for a couple of centuries or more the language of the upper classes had been French. Significantly, the Parliament Rolls were still recorded in French for many years after the nobility had learned to cope with English. It was only in the later Middle Ages that a vernacular literature began to re-emerge.

The Reformation helped the development of an English culture and intellectual tradition. This was most obvious in poetry and drama in the sixteenth century, although it led on to the remarkable scientific and philosophical speculation which was a feature of Britain in the seventeenth century. Of course, some of this might have happened anyway, but the Reformation certainly removed some impediment to speculation, and ensured that much of the intellectual discourse was within a native English/British context. Not that Britain was cut off from intellectual currents in Europe. There was still a European community of scholars, well aware of each other's work. But within that community there was emerging a distinctive British tradition of thought.

This developing national culture was paralleled by the growth of nationalist sentiment, clearly evident in Shakespeare's plays. English nationalism was established so relatively early compared with its development elsewhere that its presence has become subliminal in the national consciousness. In later centuries it hardly needed to be crudely asserted, because English nationhood was an incontrovertible fact, unlike German, Italian, Polish or Czech nationhood. Yet nationalism has been and remains an important constituent of modern British political ideologies – most obviously of conservatism, which has successfully hijacked nationalist symbols for party purposes, but also for British liberalism and labourism. Within liberalism there was long a tension between internationalist ideals and national interests – notably in the division between the Liberal imperialists and pro-Boers at the turn of the century, while British socialism or labourism has been markedly insular and infected by nationalist assumptions. It was perhaps also the early emergence of English national sentiment which has made British nationalism a somewhat partial and questionable enterprise. Possibly because the notion of 'Britain' is so difficult to disentangle from the notion of 'England', it has never commanded the universal allegiance of Scots and Welsh, whose own nationalism is in part a reaction against an English nationalism that is no less real for being expressed through cultural and economic hegemony, rather than articulated in overtly political form.

These were among the long-term political consequences of the English Reformation. The more immediate political implications of the Reformation were both profound and contradictory. On the one hand it confirmed and extended what has come to be called the 'Tudor despotism'. On the other it unleashed subversive forces which were ultimately to destroy that despotism.

In making the breach with Rome, Henry VIII had made a dramatic assertion of royal power as well as national sovereign independence. The English Reformation was initially imposed from the top for what might euphemistically be called reasons of state. Yet the relative triviality of the king's original motivation only serves to underline the apparently total nature of the authority which he wielded. He had firmly subordinated the power of the Church to the secular power of the monarchy. He was to be the head of the Church, the disposer of its wealth, and the arbiter of its doctrines. All this paved the way for what Dickens (1959) termed a 'lay-dominated society', and what Elton (1953) described as the 'Tudor Revolution in Government'. Henry had apparently laid the foundations for an absolutism which was unknown to his medieval predecessors, but which was to become only too familiar over much of Europe in the next two centuries.

Nevertheless, the Reformation also unleashed intellectual currents which the royal power found difficult to control. Henry VIII was not mainly actuated by religious conviction, but he had aligned himself with Protestant currents of thought on the continent which had already proved potentially politically subversive. Many Protestants wanted more than the substitution of royal power for papal power on questions of religious belief and observance. Their convictions were to plague Henry VIII's Tudor and Stuart successors.

Furthermore, if the spiritual authority of popes and priests could be questioned and overturned, similar questions could be asked of secular power. A direct relationship between the believer and God, without the necessary intermediary of an ecclesiastical hierarchy, was a notion which was corrosive of authority and hierarchy in general. This was a point which the Elizabethan divine, Richard Hooker (1554–1600), fully realised. If individual conscience was to be the only guide and restraint on matters of faith and conduct, then the result, he argued, would be anarchy. James I made a similar point more succinctly in expressing his opposition to Presbyterianism – 'No bishop, no king.' Freedom of conscience in matters of religious faith would breed scepticism towards secular authority (Hill, 1980, ch. 5).

It was not surprising, then, that Puritans figured prominently in the parliamentary opposition to Elizabeth and the early Stuarts, nor that some Puritans later embraced republicanism, and a few egalitarian principles. Individual liberty of conscience in religion therefore implied a similar individualism or liberalism on political questions. For those on the other side, like Hooker, the claims of authority in religious matters were bound up inseparably with political authority and social hierarchy. The connection was to be powerfully demonstrated in the seventeenth century.

The English Civil War and the Glorious Revolution

The legacy of the seventeenth century is rather more obvious for British political ideologies than the Reformation. After all, the period saw the emergence of the Whig and Tory parties, key features of the modern British Constitution, and a ferment of political ideas, many of which have an enduring significance. It will also be argued that there was a negative as well as a positive legacy. The rejection of revolution and 'extremism' and the preference for gradualism and the politics of pragmatism and compromise, which many would see as a marked feature of British political culture, is perhaps the most important consequence of the conflicts of the seventeenth century. Similarly, the virtual absence of republicanism in modern British politics is in marked contrast with its fashionableness for a time in the seventeenth century, and these features are hardly unconnected.

What has been described here as the positive legacy of the seventeenth century is possibly more contentious than it once was. There is, unsurprisingly, substantial disagreement among historians over the causes of the Civil War and its essential nature. In Britain there was for a long time a dominant Whig interpretation of seventeenth- and eighteenth-century history. It is only more recently that the ideological assumptions behind the Whig interpretation of history have been recognised and challenged. But it does not follow that more recent interpretations have successfully stripped away the distortions imposed by ideological assumptions and restored some kind of unvarnished truth. The writing of history inevitably involves selection and emphasis which reflect presuppositions and ideological assumptions in the author.

Essentially, Whig historians saw the seventeenth century in terms of an ultimately successful struggle by Parliament on behalf of the people against royal absolutism. This struggle established the sovereignty of Parliament, the principle of government by consent, religious toleration, and the balanced British Constitution. All this provided the very foundation of British freedom and prosperity.

This was history viewed with the benefit of hindsight of later constitutional developments, and history written by the victors from their own distinctive ideological perspective. This view of history was subsequently challenged by 'revisionists' who declined to see seventeenth-century political upheavals in terms of clear conflicts between opposed principles. The early seventeenth century, they suggested, was rather a period of ideological consensus, with leading Parliamentarians sharing the constitutional convictions of the Stuarts. It has even been argued that in some respects it was the opponents of Charles I who were the real reactionaries, while the policies of the king and his advisers, Laud and Strafford, were enlightened and progressive. This revisionist version of seventeenth-century history has been challenged in its turn from a variety of perspectives (Cust and Hughes, 1989).

Here we are concerned essentially with the impact of the seventeenth-century political upheavals on the British political tradition, and in that context it might be suggested that myth is more important than reality. The Whig interpretation may have become partially discredited among historians, yet it has seeped into later British thinking about politics.

If the motives of the protagonists are ignored, and the actual outcome of these political upheavals is considered, there remains surely an element of truth in the Whig interpretation. Clearly, the seventeenth century, in retrospect at least, saw the end of any prospect of establishing a royal absolutism – and this marked off the British political tradition from developments over most of the continent of Europe. Elsewhere, the authority of kings and princes was maintained and enhanced – so that it has become customary to talk of an age of absolutism. Significantly many of the reform-minded thinkers of the eighteenth-century Enlightenment on the continent sought change from above rather than below, and met with some superficial response from the 'benevolent despots' who flattered them with their attention.

In Britain the monarchy survived, but royal power progressively declined. The idea of absolutism has virtually disappeared from British political discourse since the seventeenth century. But during most of the seventeenth century, the whole issue of royal authority was very much alive and endlessly debated. Royalists now had to demonstrate and justify what had previously been taken for granted. Filmer (1588–1603), for example, attempted to buttress the royalist cause by supplementing the familiar argument for the divine right of kings with a patriarchal analogy derived from Aristotle. Hobbes (1588–1679), by contrast, ignored these traditional arguments. His justification for yielding unconditional obedience to the sovereign power was ultimately utilitarian – because of the peace and security which the sovereign could supply. Yet although Hobbes was convinced that he had found a surer basis for authority, his ideas were unpopular with the royalists, who burnt his books and tried to secure his prosecution for atheism. It is not difficult to see why. His arguments justified obedience to any sovereign who was able to deliver peace and security – to an Oliver Cromwell, or in theory at least, to a sovereign Parliament. But both Hobbes and his royalist critics were on the losing side. It was other ideas which won the day and became embedded in British political thinking.

Hobbes had preached virtually unconditional obedience to the sovereign power, while the contrary ideas of limited government and government by consent gained ground and became implicit, and to a degree explicit, in the post-1688 revolutionary settlement. Hobbes had also taught that sovereignty, or supreme power, cannot be divided, while Locke (1632–1704) and others suggested that it not only could be divided, but should be. The idea of the balanced constitution and the separation of powers, anathema to Hobbes, was soon widely associated with the British political system, both by domestic and foreign commentators. Of course, it might be suggested that such ideas were imperfectly realised in practice, and that the legal principle of the sovereignty of Parliament, or the actual political dominance of the cabinet indicates that sovereignty was effectively concentrated. Yet for all this, the idea of the balanced constitution and government by consent became part of the British political tradition. Although in origin Whig, it permeated virtually all subsequent political thought, including conservatism.

Significantly, British right-wing ideas have not been reactionary in the sense that the French right was reactionary. The Tories, and later Conservatives, remained essentially the party of monarchy, but of constitutional monarchy. They accepted limitations on the authority of government, and most of them even changes in the dynasty. They have not been 'ultras' defending fundamental principles. Compromise, gradualism and an acceptance of change have been more generally the hallmarks of British conservatism in action.

If the seventeenth century destroyed royal absolutism, it also ultimately established religious pluralism and a degree of cultural diversity. It took a century and a half after the English Reformation to confirm finally that the old orthodoxy would not be re-established, nor effectively replaced by a new uniformity, even though it required another century and a half before dissenters and Catholics were freed from their civil disabilities. Religious toleration was finally if reluctantly conceded on virtually all sides as a matter of practical necessity, and subsequently became a key point of political principle, generally if not universally accepted.

Effectively, the seventeenth century confirmed and extended the individualism which was always perhaps implicit in the Protestant Reformation. In this, Hobbes and Locke, who were at odds on so much else, were at one. Social behaviour could only be understood in terms of individual psychology and motivation. Society was essentially just an aggregate of individuals – so much so indeed, that it had to be artificially created. Both Hobbes and Locke used the notion of a contract to establish a society and government, although neither of course invented the idea which had been current for some time. The notion of rational self-seeking individuals underpinned their assumptions over the origins and development of civil society and government, and was the explicit premiss behind their entire political theory.

Such individualist assumptions fitted easily with an empirical, sceptical mode of thinking, which became the hallmark of the British philosophical and political tradition. Scepticism over ultimate truths and values and a rejection of authority entailed a relativism and an absence of fanaticism (or principle depending on one's point of view) which has permeated all mainstream British political ideologies.

Religious diversity was paralleled by a degree of political diversity, in the sense that the existence of rival political parties or factions with different personnel, ideas and interests was, albeit reluctantly, accepted. The Whig and Tory Parties originated in the seventeenth century. Recent historians have effectively destroyed the old portrayal of pre-nineteenth-century political history in terms of a two-party conflict, yet the further implication that the terms 'Whig' and 'Tory' were virtually devoid of meaning is surely going too far. While they involved nothing like modern political parties, they clearly implied distinct political outlooks to contemporaries, even if there were inevitably subtle shifts in Whiggism and Toryism over the years. British politics in the eighteenth century did involve, to a degree, a choice of men and measures. Opposition, from being regarded as at best factious and at worst treasonable, became legitimate. 'Outs' could hope to become 'Ins', at least within reason.

For of course, the political conflict which was now accepted was within fairly clear limits. Certain views and perspectives were beyond the pale. The Restoration in 1660 had effectively narrowed the scope of political debate. Views which had been vigorously canvassed and, indeed, widely held only a few years before, such as the radical democratic and embryo socialist ideas of the Levellers and Diggers, were henceforth proscribed and effectively excluded from serious political dialogue. They never completely disappeared, but went underground – to resurface occasionally in subsequent abortive rebellions, risings, disturbances and plots in the late seventeenth, eighteenth and early nineteenth centuries – but they were outside the mainstream British political tradition.

A clear example is republicanism, which was a vigorous creed among the political classes of the mid-seventeenth century. It is an obvious point, but one which requires emphasis, that a king was beheaded in England, and a republic established, a full 140 years

The New Liberalism

The 'New Liberalism' which developed from the late nineteenth century has been the subject of intense controversy. For the new liberals themselves, such as L. T. Hobhouse, who wrote a seminal text on *Liberalism* in 1911, the New Liberalism developed naturally out of the old, extending and refining familiar liberal principles and concepts. But for some Liberals at the time the new ideas seemed more a betrayal than a development of liberalism, a view echoed by modern neo-liberal critics, who identify liberalism with free market economics. For Gray the 'revisionist liberalism' of the late nineteenth and early twentieth centuries was but the culmination of 'anti-liberal elements' which 'began to enter the liberal tradition itself from the mid-1840s in the work of John Stuart Mill' (Gray, 1986, p. 33). For radical and socialist critics on the other hand, the New Liberalism has been dismissed as a forlorn attempt to revive and update an outmoded ideology (Arblaster, 1984, ch. 16).

The origins of the New Liberalism have been variously explained. Intellectually, it has been ascribed to the influence of Hegelian idealism on British liberal thinkers (Pearson and Williams, 1984, p. 146). At the level of party politics, it has been seen in terms of the need to attract working-class votes, and head off the rising challenge from labour, with both a small and large 'l'. At the level of public policy, it has been viewed as a project to modernise the British economy and society, and enable Britain to compete more effectively in the world economy and maintain its status as the leading imperial power (Hay, 1983).

To an extent the New Liberalism can be seen, however, as a *post hoc* rationalisation of the substantial growth in government intervention which had been taking place throughout the Victorian period, much of it actively promoted by Liberal governments at national level and committed Liberal supporters at local level. In the debate over the New Liberalism, rather too much emphasis has been placed on the welfare reforms of the 1906–14 Liberal government, as if these involved a quite radical departure from previous Liberal practice, when previous Whig and Liberal governments had involved considerable state intervention.

At local level, the involvement of Liberals in interventionist policies in the Victorian period is even more apparent. Here, there were fewer intellectual inhibitions over collectivist ideas.

Enthusiasm for a whole range of publicly inspired civic improvements amounted to a 'municipal gospel'. Radical liberals saw city government as a testbed for policies which could be applied nationally.

A key figure here was Joseph Chamberlain (1836–1914), who made his name as a radical Liberal mayor of Birmingham before making a successful transition to the national political scene. His campaign for the 'Unauthorised Programme' in 1885 drew extensively on his own local government experience. 'The experience of the great towns is very encouraging,' he urged:

> By their wise and liberal use of the powers entrusted to them, they have, in the majority of cases, protected the health of the community; they have provided means of recreation and enjoyment and instruction, and they have done a great deal to equalise social advantages. . . . You have, in connection with the great municipal corporations, hospitals, schools, museums, free libraries, art galleries, baths, parks. All these things which a generation ago could only have been obtained by the well-to-do, are now, in many large towns, placed at the service of every citizen by the action of the municipalities. (Speech at Hull, 1885, quoted in Schultz, 1972, pp. 57–8)

At Warrington in the same year Chamberlain explicitly rejected the principles of *laissez-faire*. The problem of poverty was, he said, one which 'some men would put aside by reference to the eternal laws of supply and demand, to the necessity of freedom and contract, and to the sanctity of every private right of property. But, gentlemen, these phrases are the convenient cant of selfish wealth. . . . These are no answers to our questions.' He went on to brush aside allegations that what he was advocating involved socialism. 'Of course it is Socialism. The Poor Law is Socialism. The Education Act is Socialism. The greater part of municipal work is Socialism, and every kindly act of legislation by which the community has sought to discharge its responsibilities and its obligations to the poor is Socialism, but is none the worse for that (quoted in Schultz, 1972, pp. 58–9)

Chamberlain's subsequent split with Gladstone and later career as a Liberal Unionist member of Tory governments has made his relationship to the liberal tradition somewhat ambivalent and contentious. But as a radical liberal with roots in local government, Chamberlain was only the most prominent of a whole new breed of

liberals who were coming to prominence in the party in the late nineteenth century. The radical, reforming approach of the Unauthorised Programme was echoed in the Newcastle programme, and culminated in the social welfare reforms of Asquith, Lloyd George and Churchill.

In this context New Liberal ideas were not some alien transplant from German philosophy. Hegelian idealism was in truth a rather exaggerated influence on New Liberal thought. T. H. Green (1836–82) admittedly derived his 'political obligations' from Kant and Hegel, but not all New Liberals were idealists and not all idealists were liberals. Perhaps the most important of all the New Liberal thinkers, Leonard Hobhouse (1864–1929), was a noted critic of what he termed 'The Metaphysical Theory of the State' (1918). More significant was the influence of earlier British liberals such as Mill, and the developing practice of liberalism at national and more particularly local level. T. H. Green was a local councillor as well as an Oxford philosopher, and well aware of municipal powers and achievements.

The New Liberals were essentially engaged in an extensive project to redefine old liberal concepts and values in line with new political practice. Freedom for Green meant 'a positive power or capacity of doing or enjoying something worth doing or enjoying'. 'The ideal of true freedom is the maximum of power for all members of human society alike to make the best of themselves.' Individual liberty remained the touchstone of liberalism, but the New Liberalism, according to Hobson involved 'a fuller realisation of individual liberty contained in the provision of equal opportunities for self-development' (Hobson, quoted in Eccleshall, 1986, p. 204). Self-development was a key concept which had links with John Stuart Mill and Gladstonian liberalism, but for the New Liberals it could be used to justify state intervention – to remove barriers to self-development. However, 'Liberals must ever insist that each enlargement of the authority and functions of the State must justify itself as an enlargement of personal liberty, interfering with individuals only in order to set free new and larger opportunities.' (Hobson, quoted in Eccleshall, 1986, p. 206)

Such caveats were, however, quite consistent with extensive programmes of state action. Another New Liberal, D. G. Ritchie (1853–1903) suggested that 'the means of communication and locomotion can in every civilised country be easily nationalised or

municipalised, where this has not been done already.' Although 'with regard to productive industries there may appear greater difficulty', Ritchie reckoned that the development of 'enormous jointstock companies, worked by salaried managers' would make the 'transition to management by government (central or local) very much more simple and very much more necessary'. The state would 'substitute for the irresponsible company or trust the responsible public corporation' (quoted in Schultz, 1972, pp. 75–7).

Hobhouse was prepared to justify extensive interference with the market to secure 'the right to work' and 'the right to a living wage'. There was, he argued, 'a defect in the social system, a hitch in the economic machine'. Individual action is here fruitless. 'The individual workman cannot put the machine straight. . . . He does not direct and regulate industry. He is not responsible for its ups and downs, but he has to pay for them.' (Hobhouse, 1911, pp. 83–4)

Liberal politicians were not always prepared to go as far as these New Liberal ideologues, but the record of the 1906–14 Liberal government included the provision of school meals, old age pensions, health and unemployment insurance, labour exchanges and progressive taxation. There was a readiness to promote state welfare provision, intervene in the operations of the labour market, and secure some modest redistribution of income and wealth (Fraser, 1984, ch. 7). But these measures by themselves did not involve a radical transformation of the old liberal ideology. Rather, they were the culmination of a trend which had begun in the early nineteenth century. The academic debate over the degree of influence of the New Liberal thinkers on Liberal policy is rather beside the point. There was rather a two-way process in which practice forced some reconsideration of theory, and this in turn helped provide a justification for further reform.

The extent to which the New Liberalism was the product of changing class forces is another interesting but ultimately rather fruitless debate. Undoubtedly, Liberal politicians were concerned about the 'rising challenge of labour', and it was hoped by some leading Liberals that social reforms would win votes. Others feared they could be an electoral liability. Radical commitments might not win working-class votes, but could easily alienate the middle classes. Rosebery was convinced that the detailed promises contained in the Newcastle programme had cost the party support (Bernstein, 1986, ch. 2). It was a factor in his Liberal Imperialism

and his commitment to the National Efficiency movement which could appeal both to a chauvinistic working class, and progressive businessmen interested in modernisation. In this context, social welfare reforms could be dressed up as good for business, and good for the British empire. Later historians have disagreed over the electoral appeal of state welfare. While welfare reforms were advocated by leaders of the organised working class, they were not necessarily popular with working-class voters.

The New Liberalism ultimately failed to prevent the decline of the Liberal Party. Whether this rapid decline into virtual political oblivion was inevitable is an interesting although speculative question on which historians have disagreed (Dangerfield, 1970; Clarke, 1971, ch. 15). However, New Liberal thinking did not share the fate of the party. On the contrary, and rather ironically, the culmination of New Liberal thought can be seen in the social welfare proposals of Beveridge and the economic theory of Keynes which provided the basis of the post-Second World War consensus accepted by the leadership of the Labour and Conservative Parties.

Keynes and Beveridge were both large 'L' as well as small 'l' liberals. Beveridge had been strongly influenced by the New Liberal thinking of his youth and had played a role in the establishment of Churchill's Labour Exchanges in the 1906–14 Liberal government. Keynes had made a major contribution to Lloyd George's election programme in 1929. Although their ideas have been claimed for social democracy, they were essentially in the liberal tradition, particularly the progressive New Liberal tradition. The Beveridge Report was based on the insurance principle, and although far more comprehensive, was in keeping with the spirit of the Lloyd George insurance scheme of 1911. Keynes's economic theory involved government intervention at the macroeconomic level, but this removed the necessity for detailed intervention in particular sectors of the economy or industries. Essentially capitalism would be managed in a way which would continue to allow markets to operate freely at the micro-level. Neither Beveridge nor Keynes saw any need for an end to the private ownership of the means of production. It was precisely this kind of state intervention to promote employment and welfare provision, but short of socialism, which was favoured by earlier New Liberals like Green and Hobhouse (George and Wilding, 1980).

Neo-liberalism

The Keynes–Beveridge post-war consensus was finally shattered, in part by a revival in classical economic liberalism, commonly referred to as 'neo-liberalism', which, although only one letter removed from New Liberalism is far apart on the ideological spectrum. The most obvious feature of neo-liberalism is support for free market principles and almost total opposition to government intervention in the economic and social spheres. The key thinker is Hayek, although a number of other writers have been claimed for this neo-liberal revival with varying degrees of plausibility, including Popper, Talmon, Berlin, Rawls, Nozick, Friedman and Buchanan (Gray, 1986, ch. 5). In Britain, neo-liberal ideas have been advanced by such bodies as the Institute of Economic Affairs and the Adam Smith Institute, and have been particularly influential within the Thatcher government. Indeed, it has been suggested by Milton Friedman, that Mrs Thatcher is essentially a nineteenth-century liberal. The debate on what has come to be called 'Thatcherism', and its relationship to neo-liberalism will be explored in the context of conservatism (see Chapter 4). Here it is only necessary to point out that fashionable neo-liberal thinkers have provoked a considerable reinterpretation of the earlier history of liberalism.

Some modern accounts of liberalism by neo-liberals dismiss, ignore or reject a century or more of evolution in British liberal thought and policy, and redefine liberalism exclusively in terms of a rather narrow and one-sided view of classical liberalism (Gray, 1986; Barry, 1986). Friedrich Hayek perhaps started this reinterpretation. He rejected not only the New Liberalism but also a substantial strand of classical liberalism in condemning the 'constructivist rationalism' of the English Utilitarians and others (Hayek, 1975).

Twentieth-century radical and Marxist commentators on liberalism have also tended to elevate the importance of particular thinkers such as Malthus, Cobden and Spencer, and rely on a somewhat selective interpretation of others such as Bentham and Mill, because it fits their general critique. In many ways this provides a valuable corrective to the rosy picture of the liberal tradition provided by liberal sympathisers, but it unfortunately tends to reinforce the one-sided neo-liberal view of liberal ideology. Such critics are rather too ready to accept the claims of the neo-liberals that theirs is the true liberalism, and that other brands are heresies or aberrations.

Arblaster (1984) for example is dismissive of the New Liberalism (which is described with the addition of a question mark) and clearly regards the neo-liberal revival as more central to liberal philosophy than the development of British Liberalism over the last 100 years.

There is surely a problem with such a narrow view of liberalism. The modern British Liberal Party may perhaps be dismissed as an irrelevance, although a definition of liberalism which appears to exclude entirely the Liberalism practised by the party of that name in this country over the last century raises certain questions. But it is not just the New Liberalism and its legacy which is rejected, but the radicalism of Paine, and the utilitarianism of Bentham and Mill. Moreover, the emphasis on the economic ideas of the classical economists tends to downplay the importance of the Whig tradition and the liberal Nonconformist conscience to British liberalism. Religious dissent, political reform, and a distinctive attitude to international affairs were the driving forces behind Gladstonian Liberalism. These were the issues of principle which united and divided politicians, which prompted resignations and party splits, and which inflamed popular passions. Arguments over state intervention involved appeals to economic principles, but tended to be resolved pragmatically. Interpretations of British liberalism wholly or largely in terms of *laissez-faire* economics involve a substantial distortion of history.

Liberalism today

What then is the present position of liberalism in Britain today, and what are its prospects? It was suggested at the beginning of this chapter that all modern British political ideologies could be seen as in some sense variants of liberalism. The term 'liberal' is still extensively employed in modern political vocabulary, and can only be invested with some precision by qualifying it. To describe a politician or a writer or a policy as 'liberal' is profoundly unhelpful, unless some modifying adjective or prefix is employed. There are neo-liberals, market liberals or economic liberals, who favour free market ideas and are generally regarded as on the right of the political spectrum. Indeed, quite a few combine economic liberalism with distinctively conservative views on social issues and problems. On the other hand, there are progressive or social liberals

who are enthusiastic about penal reform, civil liberties, the protection of the rights of minorities, freedom of expression and open government, who are unashamed interventionists in the economic sphere. Those who, like Samuel Brittan, regard themselves as both economic and social liberals are relatively unusual.

Among all these varieties of liberals there remains the British Liberal Party, and its more recent successor the Social and Liberal Democrats, who would still regard themselves as the only true heirs of the liberalism of Gladstone, Mill and Lloyd George, and the only credible vehicle for the promotion and development of liberal ideology. The revival of the British Liberal Party from the 1960s onwards, first alone, and then in alliance with the Social Democratic Party (SDP), might be taken as some indication of the support for liberalism, but this seems questionable. The considerable support the party attracted in key parliamentary by-elections, local elections, and up to a point in General Elections, was volatile and unreliable. Much of it does seem to have been a negative vote against the major parties, rather than a positive vote for Liberalism.

Liberal Party policy in the post-war period has been comfortably within the New Liberal tradition – welfare capitalism with a strong emphasis on individual rights. Distinctive Liberal policies have included early advocacy of UK entry into the EEC, devolution, incomes policies, partnership in industry, electoral reform (sometimes as part of a package of constitutional reform), and a focus on the community (Tivey and Wright, 1989, pp. 83–6). This last element has been closely linked with Liberal successes in local government, where the party has enjoyed a taste of power. At national level it has adopted an intermediate position between the two major parties, closer to the Conservatives on trade unionism, and closer to Labour on defence and foreign affairs. Its internationalist stance on foreign policy questions can be said to follow the tradition established by Bright and Gladstone.

Whether the post-war British Liberal Party has really done anything to extend or develop liberalism may be doubted, however. The party has been fertile in policy proposals but has not come up with any startling new ideas or major thinkers. Neither its electoral successes nor its failures seeem to have owed much to liberal ideology. The crucial decisions with which its leadership has been faced have been tactical rather than ideological – whether to accept Heath's offer of a coalition in 1974, whether to support the Labour

government after 1977, how to handle the SDP breakaway from Labour after 1981, and how soon and how fast to promote a merger with the SDP. All these decisions, of course, have had important ideological implications, but they were not ideologically driven.

In fact there has been rather more intellectual ferment among the modern Liberal Party's uneasy allies, the SDP, and their post-merger remnants. It could be argued that the dividing line between New Liberalism and Fabian socialism or labourism was always a thin one. (Hobhouse after all talked of liberal socialism in 1911 while Hobson made the transition to Labour following the First World War.) That line has perhaps grown thinner still as a consequence of revisionist tendencies on the right of the Labour Party in the 1950s, and the SDP breakaway in the 1980s. In this context, the Liberal/SDP Alliance and subsequent merger can be seen as the practical expression of an ideological convergence which was already well under way (Behrens, 1989). To this degree, social democrats like David Marquand, or, retrospectively and more questionably, revisionist socialists like Anthony Crosland, could be claimed for liberalism. But Liberals have reacted rather cautiously to the spate of new social democratic writing and thinking. Bradley (1985) quotes Michael Meadowcroft's warning that 'the SDP is at one and the same time the greatest opportunity and the greatest danger to liberalism for 30 years.' Bradley's main interest in this social democratic literature seems to be in the extent to which socialism is repudiated and liberal ideas embraced. He suggests, rather unprophetically, that the second edition of David Owen's *Face the Future* marks 'the beginning of a process of "liberalisation"' for the Social Democrats' (Bradley, 1985, p. 172).

On the other hand, it could be said that the shifting prospects of the modern successors of the old Liberal Party, with or without their recent allies, are a poor indication of the state of liberalism in Britain today. Eccleshall goes as far as to say 'There is a sense in which it is not misleading to suggest that the disintegration of the Liberal Party signifies the triumph of liberalism.' He points out that 'liberalism has been vulnerable to ideological pillage from its inception', and concludes, 'If liberalism is now partly invisible, this is because so many of its assumptions and ideals have infiltrated political practice and current awareness' (Eccleshall, 1986, p. 56).

There is an obvious sense in which this is true. Many of the specific proposals put forward by liberals in the past, including

proposals which seemed once radical or even revolutionary, such as universal suffrage, a range of welfare reforms, and government management of the economy have long been put into practice, and absorbed into British political culture. Moreover, a number of legislative changes in the 1960s, including divorce, homosexual and abortion law reform, and some relaxation of censorship, went a long way towards the implementation of the principles of individual liberty announced by John Stuart Mill in 1859. Subsequent legislation on equal pay, equal opportunities, and race and sex discrimination in the 1970s is also thoroughly consistent with liberal ideology. Such measures have been supported by modern Liberals, but have been advanced by a broad coalition of progressive opinion covering substantial elements in the Labour and Conservative Parties. A more recent progressive cause which is even more central to liberal ideology is constitutional reform. Campaigns for civil liberties and more open government, and the considerable impact made by the pressure group Charter '88, are thoroughly in keeping with the liberal tradition, and may be seen as an indication of its modern health and vitality.

At another level, however, it may be doubted how far liberal ideas have really thoroughly permeated modern British society. Much of the liberal legislation on homosexuality, equal opportunities and race and sex discrimination was stimulated by widespread evidence of intolerance, discrimination and persecution, and has provoked a formidable backlash in its turn. In fact, one fashionable interpretation of the success of 'Thatcherism' is that its neo-conservative or authoritarian populist elements have made palatable its abstruse or repugnant free market elements (Edgar, 1984; Hall and Jacques, 1983). In other words, it is its chauvinism, and tough line on immigration, law and order, and defence which have won working-class votes, not its neo-liberal economics. On this interpretation, the progressive liberal orthodoxy of the 1950s and 1960s was essentially an establishment phenomenon. The 'hangers and floggers' attending Conservative Party conferences, and the London dockers who marched in support of Powell, were possibly closer to the political views of the masses than the liberal progressive leadership of both major parties.

Others would suggest that the failure of 'progressive liberalism' to achieve a more tolerant, fair and equal society is rooted in the inadequacies of liberal ideology, that the emphasis on civil and

liberalism this freedom from constraint entailed firm limits to the power of government to interfere with individual liberty.

An important application of this was the principle of toleration. This particularly applied initially to religious belief and observance and was vigorously championed by Locke (1689). It was to receive its most eloquent expression from John Stuart Mill (1859), who used the negative conception of liberty to demand full freedom of thought and expression.

Subsequently, some liberals emphasised the freedom to enjoy certain benefits, a more positive conception of liberty which might entail extensive state intervention to enlarge freedom (Green, 1881; Hobhouse, 1911; Berlin, 1967). The conflict between these two sharply contrasting views of freedom, and their widely divergent practical implications, has been a major theme in the development of liberalism over the last hundred or so years.

Bound up with the debate over the interpretation of liberty is a similar argument over the emphasis to be placed on equality. For if liberalism has always involved a commitment to liberty, however defined, it has also involved some egalitarian assumptions. Individual human beings are seen as in some important respects naturally equal, and it is an implicit liberal premiss that one person's preferences are not be valued more highly than those of another. There is an equality with regard to the consideration of interests. Liberals have stressed equality before the law, and equal civil and political rights, although there has not always been agreement over what these should entail in practice. Egalitarian considerations have also led many liberals to justify social provision of education and other collective provision in order to establish greater equality of opportunity.

But a commitment to an equality of worth and opportunity has generally been quite consistent with a liberal acceptance of considerable inequality of income and wealth. Indeed, liberalism has also been closely associated with a defence of private property rights as a crucial element of individual liberty. Critics of liberalism have thus tended to see the liberal commitment to equality as at best highly theoretical and at worst nakedly hypocritical (Arblaster, 1984, pp. 84–91), while even sympathetic commentators have suggested that liberals have been generally prepared to sacrifice equality to liberty.

Liberals themselves have argued that freedom entails the freedom to be unequal, but they have also tended to assume that individual liberty is not inconsistent with social justice. Liberals argued that the pursuit of rational enlightened self-interest would produce the greatest public welfare. Although liberalism is based on the assumption of self-seeking individualism, it has never involved the cynical equation of might and right. Rather, liberals have embraced the language of justice, and attempted to make it consistent with the pursuit of rational self-interest (Rawls, 1971). There is implicit in such arguments some fairly optimistic assumptions about human nature and the scope for reconciling individual and collective goals.

It is here that liberalism parts company with traditional conservatism on the one hand, and socialism on the other. Conservatives have been more pessimistic about human nature, and sceptical over enlightenment and the potential for individual rational conduct (see Chapter 4). Socialists, while sharing with liberals a more optimistic view of human nature, have not accepted that individual self-interest and social justice can be so easily reconciled (see Chapter 5).

There are some underlying problems here which will require some later elaboration and discussion. For the present, it is sufficient to note that the tension between considerations of individual liberty and the sanctity of private property on the one hand, and assumptions about equality and social justice on the other, have been a major theme in the evolution of liberal thought.

While, however, there are clearly major differences and tensions within the liberal tradition, it is not that difficult to describe liberals or liberalism in terms which would command a wide element of agreement. Stuart Hall (1986, p. 34) suggests that liberals are 'open-minded, tolerant, rational, freedom-loving people, sceptical of the claims of tradition and established authority, but strongly committed to the values of liberty, competition and individual freedom.' This is a description by a non-liberal which most liberals would probably be happy to endorse. Hall goes on to argue that nineteenth-century British liberalism 'stood for individualism in politics, civil and political rights, parliamentary government, moderate reform, limited state intervention, and a private enterprise economy.'

The Whig tradition

Liberalism in Britain grew out of the Whig tradition. It is easier perhaps to distinguish liberalism from Whiggism than it is to distinguish conservatism from Toryism, but even so, the Whig tradition slides naturally and imperceptibly into the liberal tradition, to the extent that it is not possible to mark precisely where the one ends and the other begins. Whigs originated in the seventeenth century as the party which opposed royal absolutism and championed religious dissent. The Whigs in turn were the political heirs of the religious and parliamentary opposition to the early Stuarts. Whigs supported the rights of Parliament, and sought to place limits on royal power. Writers like Locke (1632–1704) sought to ground this political programme in abstract principles. There were natural rights to life, liberty and property. Government should rest on the consent of the governed, who were ultimately justified in rebellion if their rights were infringed. There should be constitutional limits on government, and a division between the executive and legislative powers. (Locke, 1689; Dunn, 1969; Macpherson, 1962). These ideas came to be enshrined, albeit somewhat imperfectly, in the British Constitution following the Glorious Revolution of 1688. They later helped to inspire or justify the American and French Revolutions, and a radical tradition in British politics.

Yet there were always contradictory tendencies in Whiggism. Behind fine sentiments there were material interests to advance and defend. The great Whig aristocrats and their allies among the merchants and bankers sought to preserve their own power, property and privileges from a perceived threat from the crown. The massive inequalities in income and wealth in eighteenth-century England were for them unproblematic (Arblaster, 1984, ch. 8). Locke spoke for their interests in defending rights to life, liberty and property. In fact liberty was not, in the seventeenth and early eighteenth centuries, the rather abstract principle it was to become, but a word closely associated with property. This was particularly the case with its commonly used plural 'liberties', which had a connotation close to the word 'privileges' with which it was often combined (Hill, 1980, pp. 36–8).

Furthermore, the Whigs in general had no wish to spread power beyond the ranks of the propertied. Arblaster (1984, p. 169) suggests that their triumph in 1689 'resulted in political reaction', with further restrictions on the very limited right to vote and the extension of the life of Parliament from three to seven years. Hence, the constitution which they developed and defended was essentially oligarchic and conservative. Worse still, it could only apparently be successfully operated on the basis of graft, corruption and jobbery. Through the period of the Whig ascendancy in the eighteenth century, patronage greased the wheels of government. Parliamentary seats, offices under the crown and commissions in the army were bought and sold.

Power was also shamelessly exercised for the benefit of the wealthy. Prodigious fortunes were made out of war, the slave trade and India. Wealthy landowners used enclosure procedures to enrich themselves at the expense of the rural poor, and all in the name of agricultural progress. The game laws were ruthlessly enforced, as naked an example of class legislation as can be found. It is not difficult, in the face of such evidence, to conclude that there was nothing more behind the political principles of the Whigs than class interest.

Still, Whig principles were capable of a radical as well as a conservative interpretation. 'No taxation without representation', the slogan of the parliamentary opposition to the Stuarts, became the cry of the American rebels against George III, and many Whigs found it difficult to deny the justice of their case. The Declaration of Independence (1776) was based on classic Whig principles. The French Revolution was more divisive, but was initially welcomed by most leading Whigs. Despite the reaction which the subsequent course of the revolution provoked, the Whig leader Charles James Fox (1749–1806) continued to defend its principles if not always its practice, and consistently championed civil liberties in England until his death.

Perhaps it was their effective exclusion from power for the greater part of the period from 1783 to 1830, which permitted some reaffirmation and development of Whig principles. Free from the messy compromises of government, Fox's followers could proclaim their continued attachment to 'Peace, retrenchment and reform'. Parliamentary reform became a Whig cause, with unsuccessful bills introduced into Parliament in 1797 and 1810, providing some precedent for the Great Reform Bill of 1832 (Watson, 1960, pp. 361–2, 450–1). The Foxite Whigs could also claim some credit for British abolition of the slave trade, the one positive achievement of their participation in the brief 'Ministry of All the Talents' in 1807 (Watson, 1960, pp. 440–1). Moreover the traditional Whig demand for religious toleration was reaffirmed in the cause of Catholic emancipation as well as Protestant dissent.

The defection of the 'Old Whigs' and the accommodation within the Foxite remnant of the party of a new generation of radicals, such as Whitbread (1758–1815), Brougham (1778–1868) and Romilly (1757–1818), with a strong commitment to reform, helped preserve or re-establish a politically progressive Whig tradition which ultimately merged into liberalism (Watson, 1960, pp. 436–7). The 1832 Reform Act was a key element in the transition. It can be seen in one sense as the culmination of the Whig tradition. Grey, the prime minister responsible for its successful passage, had, as Fox's loyal lieutenant, personally introduced the unsuccessful Reform Bill of 1797. In another sense, the Act serves to underline the cautious, essentially conservative nature of the Whigs (Wright 1970, pp. 31–6). It was a strictly limited measure, allowing for some redistribution of parliamentary seats, and a very modest extension of the franchise, to incorporate elements of the respectable propertied middle classes.

Even so, it provided the foundation for Victorian liberalism by gradually but decisively changing the political geography of Britain. The new urban centres gained at the expense of the shires, manufacture and commerce at the expense of land. Whig aristocrats as well as Tory squires ultimately lost influence to the urban-based business and professional middle classes, and it was the latter who were to provide the effective muscle behind Victorian liberalism. Whiggery had developed in a pre-industrial age, in a predominantly rural society in which land remained the overwhelming source of wealth. It was an approach to politics which was increasingly anachronistic in an industrial capitalist society, although the Whigs remained an important but diminishing element within the Liberal coalition until the late nineteenth century.

Those who would see liberalism in terms of the economic liberalism of the classical economists tend to see the political aspects of liberalism as almost accidental by-products of free market values. Such a view involves a wilful neglect of the Whig foundations for British liberalism, for the Whig/liberal tradition of thought is essentially a political tradition, concerned with constitutional and governmental issues and questions of civil liberties. Whiggism may have served economic interests, but it was never essentially an economic doctrine. It was about parliamentary sovereignty, government by consent, freedom of conscience and religious observance, no taxation without representation, and a host of other slogans and proclaimed principles, no doubt very imperfectly applied for the most part. It was not about free trade or free markets. Whig foreign trade policy in the seventeenth and eighteenth centuries was opportunist but essentially mercantilist. The aim was to secure, through colonisation, Navigation Acts and war, as large a British share of world trade as possible.

Radicals

Alongside the Whig tradition, at times interwoven with it, at times in opposition to it, there is a radical tradition which has had a marked effect on both British liberalism and, subsequently, socialism. Yet the term 'radical tradition', if it is to be used at all, must be employed more loosely. The Whigs were bound together to a degree by considerations of party, interest, and a common intellectual heritage. Radicals tended to lack even this very loose form of association. The description 'radical' has been employed to cover a wide range of politicians, thinkers and ideas, and has rather different connotations for different periods of time.

In the early nineteenth century some radicals, such as Whitbread and Brougham, were essentially the progressive wing of the parliamentary Whig Party, although somewhat later the term 'Tory radical' was applied to reformers such as Oastler (1789–1861) and Shaftsbury (1801–85). Also in touch with progressive Whig circles were the 'philosophical radicals' or utilitarians – Bentham and his followers. Then there were radicals with a substantial popular following who were distrusted or persecuted by the political establishment, like Cartwright or Hunt, and some who might be classified as revolutionaries, of whom Thomas Paine was the most significant. More difficult to classify is William Cobbett (1763–1835), initially an arch critic, and later a champion of Paine. Yet Cobbett's radical populism was always essentially harking back to a pre-industrial age. Very different was the radicalism of the Quaker manufacturer Bright, who belonged to the new generation of politicians who came to the fore after the 1832 Reform Act, and who in some ways personified the new age. However, Bright in turn lived long enough to be displaced by a new breed of radicals who took over the Liberal Party in the latter part of the century, by which time the term 'radicalism' was beginning to be associated with socialism.

Although the label is so diffuse and imprecise, it is impossible to ignore the influence of radicalism on the nineteenth-century British Liberal Party, and British liberalism more generally. At the parliamentary level, the boundary line between Whigs and radicals was shifting and imprecise. A succession of radical *enfants terribles* were subsequently incorporated into the Whig (and later Liberal) political establishment. At the popular level, radical ideas often enjoyed sufficient support to force concessions from that establishment. And ideas which were rejected as heretical or even treasonable by one generation, often became another's established orthodoxy.

It was indeed radicals both inside and outside the loose Whig parliamentary grouping which provided the dynamic element in the Whig/liberal tradition of thought. Although the mainstream Whig politicians of the eighteenth and early nineteenth centuries tended to interpret their proclaimed principles in ways which preserved their own power, property and privileges, it was always possible to give these same principles a far more radical interpretation, as Thomas Paine (1737–1809) did.

In one sense, all Paine did was to take the ideas behind the 1688 revolution, which had been proclaimed by Locke, to their logical conclusion. Once ultimate sovereignty had been transferred from the monarchy to the people, once political equality had been accepted in theory, there was no logical case for restricting participation in the choice of a legislature. Paine himself had earlier accepted some property qualification for voting, but later championed full manhood suffrage (Paine 1791–2). His contemporary, Mary Wollstonecraft (1759–97), went further in demanding full political rights for women, as well as men (Wollstonecraft, 1792). Although by turns reviled or neglected in Britain, their ideas were the logical outcome of Whig slogans. Indeed, it can be argued that the only coherent way to counter such a revolutionary democratic ideology was by assailing its egalitarian and rationalistic assumptions, as Burke realised.

Whether Paine belongs best within the British liberal or socialist tradition is a somewhat academic point. Recent editors of his work have suggested 'his political theory was vintage liberalism', citing his uncompromising individualism, his sympathies for manufacturers, and his hostility to government (Foot and Kramnick, 1987, pp. 22–9). Ayer (1988, ch. 7), by contrast, talks of 'Paine's blueprint . . . for his Welfare State', and stresses his support for a highly redistributive graduated income tax.

Paine's direct influence on British liberalism was less than the quality and the quantity of his writing perhaps deserved. There were various reasons for this. As a cosmopolitan individual whose ideas had more immediate impact in America and France than Britain, he transcended the parochial British Whig/liberal tradition of thought, and perhaps belongs more properly to the history of liberalism generally than British liberalism. Moreover, his uncompromising republicanism, his total opposition to the hereditary principle, and his opposition to Christianity, coupled with the vigorous rhetoric in which his ideas were expressed, gave him a wild and dangerous reputation. Although his immediate political influence on ruling circles in Britain was consequently negligible, and although he has had little obvious influence on subsequent mainstream British liberal thought, nevertheless, his indirect influence was arguably considerable. His writing enjoyed what for the time was a massive circulation, despite, or perhaps because of, the Government's efforts to suppress them. The Chartists acknowledged that his philosophy was their inspiration in their 1837 manifesto (Foot and Kramnick, 1987, p. 33). Demands articulated by the working classes and ultimately conceded, owed much to the wide if underground dissemination of the ideas of Thomas Paine.

Subsequent British radicals seem tame by comparison. However, it was radical pressure which committed the Whigs to parliamentary reform in 1832, and later kept up the pressure for further reform in the 1860s and 1880s. The association of radicalism with religious dissent in the second half of the nineteenth century imbued it with a strong moral character, and fuelled demands for non-denominational state education and disestablishment of the Church of England. Radicalism was also strongly associated with the municipal gospel and the growth of local government. At the parliamentary level, it was the fusion of Whigs and radicals which created the British Liberal Party.

After the establishment of the Liberal Party in 1859, Whigs continued to predominate in Liberal cabinets between 1859 and

1886, but at the increasingly important grassroots level, radicals predominated, and this was subsequently reflected in the composition of the parliamentary Liberal Party. The formation of the National Liberal Federation in particular signalled the gradual takeover of the Liberal Party by its radical grassroots supporters, and the increasing alienation of the remaining Whigs. A form of radicalism, always a potent element in British liberalism, thus effectively took it over. It might be noted, though, that it was a relatively restrained, religiously inspired, and peculiarly British strand of radicalism which eventually prevailed rather than the fiercely rationalist, republican and universalist radicalism of Thomas Paine.

Classical economics and utilitarianism

If the moral inspiration of Victorian liberalism was derived from radical Nonconformism, it drew intellectual sustenance from the ideas of the classical economists and the utilitarians. It was Adam Smith (1732–90), Malthus (1766–1834) and Ricardo (1772–1823) who virtually founded the modern study of economics, and established the importance of the operations of the market in the allocation and distribution of resources. It was Jeremy Bentham's (1748–1832) 'principle of utility' which was applied to a wide range of institutions and practices. Tradition and long usage were no justification in the face of Bentham's fiercely rationalist analysis. 'What use is it?' was his brutal question, cutting through the mystique in which constitutional and legal issues were generally surrounded. The 'only right and proper end of government' he declared, was 'the greatest happiness of the greatest number'.

To an extent, the classical economists and the utilitarians are difficult to separate. Both shared the individualist assumptions underpinning liberalism. Both stemmed from a similar intellectual climate – the eighteenth-century Enlightenment. There were also clear connections between them. Bentham and his associates broadly accepted the *laissez-faire* implications of the economic theories of Smith, Ricardo and Malthus, while Smith's friend and colleague, the philosopher and historian David Hume (1711–76), had earlier laid the foundations for utilitarianism. Some thinkers, like Nassau Senior (1790–1864), had a foot in both camps.

Even so, modern neo-liberal writers have identified a fundamental distinction between Benthamism and the ideas of Adam Smith, and have gone on to suggest that it is Smith and Hume, the great thinkers of the eighteenth-century Scottish Enlightenment, who represent the true spirit of liberalism (Gray, 1986, p. 24). Bentham and his followers, by contrast, are blamed for ideas which 'provided a warrant for much later illiberal interventionist policy'. Norman Barry (1986, pp. 19–21) similarly suggests that although 'Bentham is often credited with the liberal label' he is no true liberal.

It is not difficult to understand why neo-liberals opposed to state intervention should be critical of the utilitarians. Their 'greatest happiness' principle involved a potential breach with *laissez-faire* economics. It so happened that Bentham and his associates broadly agreed with Smith that the greatest happiness would be most effectively promoted by free markets, but of course the principle could equally well be employed to justify government intervention, and subsequently was, most notably by Bentham's formidable secretary and disciple, Edwin Chadwick (1800–90). Chadwick had been a key figure in the development and the administration of the harsh New Poor Law, but his later experiences in the Public Health movement converted him from an orthodox exponent of free market principles to a convinced advocate of state intervention and control in a wide range of issues surrounding water supply, sewage, and control of pollution (Finer, 1970).

Bentham himself had been converted by his friend and associate James Mill to representative democracy. If the end of government should be the greatest happiness of the greatest number, it followed that only a government which was freely and regularly elected by the governed, acting in accordance with rational self-interest, could be relied upon to promote the interests of the governed, rather than the interests of the rulers (Dinwiddy, 1989).

Democracy itself can provide a powerful spur for state intervention. There may be electoral pressures for public spending and governmental growth. Bentham, however, has other claims to be regarded as the father of modern bureaucracy. He sought to redesign the whole system of British government from top to bottom on rationalist lines, involving the appointment of professionally qualified, salaried, public officials.

The contradictory implications of Benthamite thinking can be seen clearly in that most notorious of utilitarian-influenced measures, the Poor Law Amendment Act of 1834. Its underlying assumptions were those of free market economics. Incentives must be maintained. In this context, the able-bodied poor who sought relief must be prepared to enter a workhouse, where their condition would be 'less eligible' than that of the lowest independent labourer. Yet the New Poor Law also involved a comprehensive network of new administrative areas, a new hierarchy of administrative officials, and a novel form of central control and inspection, that had rather different implications for the future.

All this explains why modern neo-liberals have reservations about the utilitarians. Hayek (1975) is critical of what he calls Bentham's 'constructivist rationalism'. Gray (1986) similarly castigates him for believing that 'social institutions can be the object of successful rational redesign', so that his utilitarianism 'had an inherent tendency to spawn policies of interventionist social engineering'. Norman Barry (1986) comments 'its central tenets stress artifice and design in the pursuit of collective ends.'

All this is fair comment, but what is unwarranted is their further suggestion that Bentham and the utilitarians do not really belong to the liberal tradition, while Smith and Hume are the fount of pure liberalism. This involves a *post hoc*, highly artificial, ideal type conception of liberalism which bears little relation to the British Whig/liberal tradition, or indeed to the historical experience of liberalism anywhere. The truth is that Bentham and his associates became directly and centrally involved in that Whig/liberal tradition, in terms of personal connections, ideas and practical influence on policy, while the connection of Hume and Smith with that same tradition is at best tangential. At the personal level, Hume wrote a history of England in which contemporaries perceived a strong Tory bias, while Adam Smith's own politics were more Tory than Whig. Ricardo, whose liberal credentials are, by contrast, unimpeachable (Weatherall, 1976), is curiously neglected by the neo-liberals (or perhaps not so curiously in view of the use to which Marx and others later put his labour theory of value).

The writings of all the major classical economists – Smith, Malthus, Ricardo, Nassau Senior, and, later, John Stuart Mill – certainly contributed significantly to Victorian liberalism. Yet their ideas were extensively vulgarised and over-simplified. While Adam Smith's 'invisible hand' provided a graphic and enduring vision of the beneficial operation of free market forces, even Smith allowed for significant exceptions. It was popularisers such as Harriet Martineau

(1802–76), Edward Baines (1774–1848) and Samuel Smiles (1812–1904) who reduced the principles of classical economics to the simple injunctions of *laissez-faire* for governments and 'self-help' for individuals.

Even so, *laissez-faire* was only one strand among many in Victorian liberalism, and public policy was never consistently informed by the principle. A series of Factory Acts, local and general Public Health Acts, and Acts to regulate the railways and banks were passed in the early Victorian period when *laissez-faire* ideas were most influential. Indeed economic historians question whether there ever was an age of *laissez-faire*.

Victorian liberalism

A political ideology is not to be identified with the history of a political party, yet there is inevitably a strong connection between particular systems of ideas and their practical political expressions. An account of British liberalism has perforce to pay some attention to the composition, support, and record of the British Liberal Party, especially during its heyday in the second half of the nineteenth century.

Although the term 'Liberal' was applied in British politics from the early nineteenth century, the British Liberal Party was not really established until 1859 when Palmerston formed an administration incorporating Whigs, radicals and former Peelite Conservatives. Even then the government in the domestic sphere at least remained more Whig than Liberal until at least the death of Palmerston in 1865, or the emergence of Gladstone (1809–98) as leader and then prime minister in 1868 (Bentley, 1984).

Gladstone himself came to seem the embodiment of Victorian liberalism. He so dominated the party that he was substantially able to shape it in his own image, but in some ways he was a strange figure for liberal canonisation. He had started his political career as a Conservative follower of Peel. Even after he followed his leader into opposition when the Repeal of the Corn Laws split the Conservative Party, his final destination was unclear, and some rapprochement with Derby and Disraeli's Conservatives seemed possible (Bentley, 1984, pp. 168–9). His pivotal role in Liberal politics after 1859 was still far from inevitable. He was also an

Anglican landowner with no past reputation as a radical in a party which was becoming increasingly associated with manufacturing, dissent, and radical reform. Gladstone was a politician who became more radical and populist with age. Furthermore and crucially, he was inspired by a Christian moral fervour, which struck a receptive chord among his Nonconformist followers. Gladstonian Liberalism became something of a moral crusade (Vincent, 1966; Adelman, 1970, pp. 6–7).

This Gladstonian Liberalism drew on several strands. Parliamentary reform was a theme derived from the Whig tradition. The advocacy of Bright and later Gladstone himself turned it into a populist cause. Proposals for a fairly modest extension of the franchise soon developed into radical Liberal demands for full manhood suffrage (Wright, 1970; Adelman, 1970).

Nonconformism also loomed large. According to the religious census of 1851 almost half of the church-going population of the country was Nonconformist, so that although the 1860s parliamentary party was 'still overwhelmingly Anglican', the Liberals were becoming 'the party of the Nonconformist conscience' (Vincent, 1966, pp. 61–2). It was these pressures which spawned the Liberation Society, which aimed at the disestablishment of the Church of England, and later the National Education League, committed to a national, free and secular system of education. The League in turn provided the model for the National Liberal Federation in 1877, which not only established a national organisation for the Liberal Party but also tipped it decisively in the direction of Nonconformism and radicalism. By the 1880s the parliamentary party as well as the party in the country was predominantly Nonconformist (Adelman, 1970).

A similar attitude to foreign policy and Ireland helped unite Gladstone with the Nonconformists. The importance of foreign affairs to British liberalism is often underestimated. It was support for liberal and nationalist movements on the continent, especially Italian unification, which was one factor which brought Palmerston's 1859 Government together, and subsequently kept it together. It was Gladstone's campaign against the Bulgarian atrocities which brought him out of premature retirement and into close collaboration with the Nonconformists. It was the religious fervour behind his mission to pacify Ireland which both split his party, but also strengthened the moral element in liberalism.

What has been called Manchester liberalism was a significant but retrospectively exaggerated element of the Liberal Party after 1859. Free trade had certainly been clearly established as a liberal principle. Cobden and Bright, the leaders of that classic pressure group campaign, the Anti-Corn Law League, had seen their cause victorious in 1846. Repeal of the Corn Laws symbolically reflected the transfer of power from the landed to the manufacturing interest which both Cobden and Bright represented. Gladstone as Chancellor of the Exchequer in Palmerston's government built on their work by abolishing a whole range of duties, while Cobden himself, although he had declined office, was allowed to negotiate personally the Anglo-French trade treaty of 1860.

Nevertheless, free trade did not entail *laissez-faire* in domestic policy. Cobden's opposition to Factory Acts in particular and government intervention in general seemed increasingly out of tune with the times. As for Bright, Vincent (1966, p. 168) claims that his 'theory of history and of politics did not derive from any abstract attachment of *laissez-faire* or political economy, or from any construction of his business interests.' Rather it was a moral and religious fervour which informed his views on economics and foreign affairs, and a detestation of 'privilege' which led him to champion parliamentary reform.

Liberal practice entailed increased state intervention. Major reforms in education, the army, the law and civil service were accomplished by Gladstone's 1868–74 administration. If the record of the 1880–85 administration was disappointing to Gladstone's radical supporters, the passing of the Third Reform Act in 1884 promised the triumph of radical demands for reform over Whig caution. Chamberlain's 'Unauthorised Programme' of 1885, and the 'Newcastle Programme' of 1891 marked a decisive shift towards radicalism in the British Liberal Party.

Behind the evolution of Liberal political practice there was a considerable development in political thinking. Subsequent interpretations of Victorian liberal ideology have concentrated particularly on the massive contributions of John Stuart Mill (1806–73), representing the progressive or revisionist tendencies in liberalism and Herbert Spencer (1820–1903), representing the more old-fashioned libertarian strand.

In most respects Mill was a thorough individualist. 'The sole end for which mankind are warranted, individually or collectively, in interfering with the liberty of action of any of their number is self-protection. . . . Over himself, over his own body and mind, the individual is sovereign' (Mill, 1859). This sounds like a plea for minimal state intervention, and in some respects it was. Mill was eloquent in denouncing censorship and arguing for full liberty of thought and expression. He was remarkably libertarian on matters of personal conduct also, and it was this concern for individuality which led him, despite his general advocacy of representative democracy, into fears over the 'tyranny of the majority'. He worried about the intolerance of public opinion and the 'despotism of custom' which he saw as a greater threat to individuality than deliberate actions by governments (Mill, 1859; 1861).

In other respects Mill allowed for considerable government intervention, despite his general espousal of the market in *Principles of Political Economy* (1848). Gray (1986, p. 30) quotes Dicey to the effect that Mill is 'a watershed thinker in the development of liberalism' from individualism to collectivism. Greenleaf (1983, p. 103) suggests he was to be a major instrument of the betrayal of traditional Liberal doctrine. But Mill did not transform Victorian liberalism; he largely mirrored it. On education, his views (for state aid, and even for limited state provision, but opposed to a general state education) were mainstream. His support for the activities of trade unions and even the sympathies he expressed for socialist ideas were increasingly familiar in radical liberal circles. Only in his support for women's rights was he in advance of his time.

Spencer, by contrast, was increasingly out of tune with the times he lived in. His thought combined *laissez-faire* economics with pre-Darwinian evolutionary theories which emphasised the survival of the fittest. There was, he maintained, 'a universal law of nature . . . that a creature not energetic enough to maintain itself must die.' Not surprisingly he was opposed to any welfare measures of the sort which the Liberal Party of his day was increasingly advocating and introducing at both local and national level. But he generally opposed almost all forms of state intervention, and even argued for the privatisation of the Royal Mint.

Just as in some circles there has been a tendency to elevate Smith and Hume at the expense of Bentham in the liberal pantheon, so there has been a similar tendency for much the same reasons to elevate Spencer at the expense of Mill (Greenleaf, 1983). There is scope for argument over the relative cogency and importance of their writing, but there can be no debate over which was the more representative or influential Victorian liberal thinker.

Liberalism, capitalism and democracy

Liberalism as a political ideology has been closely associated with the rise of industrial capitalism. It pre-eminently was the creed of the bourgeoisie, the owners of industrial and financial capital. Its political objectives involved the enfranchisement of the new middle classes and the effective transfer of political power to the major manufacturing urban centres of industrialised Britain. Its economic theory could be seen as the rationalisation of the interests of capital. Moreover, it was hardly purely coincidental that the British Liberal Party finally emerged in the 1850s, when Britain's industrial and commercial dominance was unchallenged, the British bourgeoisie supremely self-confident, and the working classes as yet largely non-unionised and unenfranchised. The relative decline of British manufacturing, and the rise of labour were part of the background to the subsequent decline of liberalism.

Furthermore, even if one goes back further to the roots of liberalism, it has been argued that Protestant dissent, and more particularly Puritanism, embodied ideas favourable to the spirit of capitalist accumulation, while the political thought of Hobbes, and more especially Locke, involved a 'possessive individualism' which was highly compatible with the mercantile capitalism of the seventeenth century (Macpherson, 1962).

Even so, British liberalism cannot be simply derived from capitalism. The leading Whig parliamentarians, who retained a substantial presence in nineteenth-century Liberal governments despite their diminishing numbers, were large landowners. Many of the rank and file Liberal activists were not manufacturers but relatively small shopkeepers and tradesmen (Vincent, 1966). And even before their progressive enfranchisement, a substantial section of the working class had attached itself to the Liberal cause. Liberalism in practice involved a coalition of class interests. Some of the causes it embraced, such as temperance, religious disestablishment, and Irish Home Rule, were only tenuously, if at all, connected with the interests of capitalism. Leading liberal thinkers, such as John Stuart Mill, Ritchie (1853–1903), Hobhouse (1864–1929), Keynes (1883–

4

Conservatism

Perspectives on conservatism

There are most of the usual problems found in interpreting any political ideology in examining conservatism, including conflicting perspectives, and changes over time. A problem which is perhaps less significant is the relationship between British conservatism, and conservatism elsewhere, if only because of the markedly insular character of the British variant. Until perhaps very recently, the influences of foreign thinkers or foreign models have been conspicuous by their absence. Yet there are also some particular difficulties in examining conservatism which are not encountered to the same degree with other ideologies.

One problem specifically associated with conservatism is that conservatives themselves commonly deny that it is an ideology (Kirk, 1982, p. xiv). Partly this reflects the pejorative connotation surrounding the term. For the conservative, socialism, communism, and possibly fascism might qualify as ideologies, but not conservatism. Conservatism is held to indicate not an elaborate system of thought, but rather an attitude of mind; not the application of some predetermined blueprint, but a common sense approach to immediate practical problems. Pragmatism is thus opposed to ideology. The Conservative Party is characterised as a pragmatic rather than an ideological party. Consequently, it is asserted, it is a mistake to expect to find consistent principles behind conservatism, which has evolved and changed in accordance with circumstances.

Critics of conservatism sometimes employ very different terminology to reach a substantially similar conclusion. Conservatism for political rights, on institutional procedures, and the redress of specific individual grievances, all grounded in individualist liberal philosophy, is not enough. Such critics would argue that it is necessary to go beyond liberalism.

government is equality of rights. Every man has a right to one vote.' (Foot and Kramnick, 1987, p. 459) James Mill not only convinced himself of the case for representative democracy, but also Jeremy Bentham, as the only sure means for promoting the 'greatest happiness of the greatest number', in advance of the Chartist campaign for adult male suffrage. John Stuart Mill argued for the extension of full political rights to women, well before there was any sustained campaign for female suffrage. Commentators have been quick to seize on any shortcomings in the commitment of these writers to democracy – the exclusion of women from James Mill's franchise, and his son's flirtation with plural voting. In so doing they ignore the substance of their support for what was then a radical minority cause.

Of course, many Whigs and liberals in the early and mid-nineteenth century did not want to go as far or as fast as these thinkers, but once the logic of the movement for parliamentary reform was accepted and British liberals became finally committed to the theory and practice of representative democracy, their conversion was wholehearted. Indeed, the arrival of 'government by the people' was seen by many liberals as a justification for abandoning former limitations to government intervention. So Chamberlain argued in 1885, 'I quite understand the reason for timidity in dealing with this question (poverty) so long as the government was merely the expression of the will of a prejudiced and limited few. . . . But now we have a Government of the people by the people . . .' (speech at Warrington, quoted in Schultz, 1972, p. 59). Ritchie in 1891 wrote that 'the explicit recognition of popular sovereignty tends to abolish the antithesis between "the Man" and "the State." The State becomes, not "I" indeed but "we"' (quoted in Schultz, 1972, p. 77). Herbert Samuel in 1902 argued that a reformed state could be entrusted with social reform. 'Now democracy has been substituted for aristocracy as the root principle of the constitution . . . the State today is held worthy to be the instrument of the community in many affairs for which the State of yesterday was clearly incompetent' (quoted in Schultz, 1972, p. 81). The acceptance of democracy thus was a critical step towards the New Liberalism. There was an inexorable logic by which liberals progressed from parliamentary reform to representative democracy, to state intervention, and the apparent abandonment of some of the principles associated with earlier liberalism.

1946) and Beveridge (1879–1963), gave only qualified support for capitalism.

The establishment of a capitalist economy was accompanied by the gradual establishment of a liberal democratic system in the United Kingdom, and this may not have been coincidental. Indeed some Marxists have argued that representative democracy affords the best shell for capitalism. If that is so, then it was hardly surprising that the party of the bourgeoisie should have been in the forefront of the parliamentary reform movement in Britain. However, it should be noted that this cause attracted not only the millowner Bright, but the Whig aristocrat Russell and the landowner Gladstone, and of course the enthusiastic support of liberal tradesmen and skilled workmen.

Of course, support for parliamentary reform in the mid-nineteenth century commonly stopped short of support for full representative democracy, and this has provided some evidence for those commentators who have denied any reciprocal tie of dependence between liberalism and democracy. Arblaster talks of the 'fear of democracy' and argues that 'middle class liberals were fearful, not only for wealth and property, but also for the position and values of their class' and concludes of parliamentary reform 'No issue has so clearly revealed the class character of liberalism as an ideology.' (Arblaster, 1964, p. 264) From a different perspective Gray identifies liberalism not with democracy, but with limited government. This, he declares, 'need not be democratic government' and proceeds to argue 'where it is unlimited, democratic government cannot be liberal government since it respects no domain of independence or liberty as being immune to invasion by governmental authority.' (Gray, 1986, p. 74)

Such verdicts involve a rather strained interpretation of the evolution of liberalism, and particularly, a neglect of its development over the last century. Democracy in the eighteenth century was a remote theoretical model, interpreted by educated Englishmen, if at all, through Thucydides, Plato and Aristotle. Representative democracy in the early nineteenth century was a largely untried system. In these circumstances it is not surprising that middle-class opinion was rather apprehensive about its possible consequences, and it is remarkable that it was advocated at all. Yet it was. Paine, whose political theory has been described as 'vintage liberalism' (Foot and Kramnick, 1987, p. 22) was (as we have seen) a consistent advocate of manhood suffrage. 'The true and only basis of representative them is essentially a ruling-class ideology, and it has evolved in accordance with the changing interests of the ruling class (Eccleshall, 1977). Conservative principles are therefore rationalisations of class interest, the defence of the status quo and existing property rights, and there is little point in seeking any more logical coherence or long-term consistency in conservatism. As one recent trenchant critic has concluded 'Selfishness is the rationale of their politics, and they have no other rationale.' (Honderich, 1990, p. 238)

Both conservatives and their critics have accordingly tended to emphasise the theme of pragmatism. Reflecting the very considerable success the British Conservative Party has enjoyed in securing outright control or dominance over government in the last hundred years or so, conservatism is presented as essentially a philosophy of government, if indeed it can be viewed as a philosophy at all.

There is something in all this, although it might be observed that while conservatism now plausibly appears as a philosophy of government or a ruling-class ideology, this was not always the case. For much of the eighteenth century, Toryism was the frustrated political expression of the 'outs' – malcontents, permanent backwoodsmen and romantic dreamers. In the mid-nineteenth century, conservatism seemed to be tied to a landed interest which was in manifest decline, and it was liberalism which seemed destined to be established as the ideology of the new emerging ruling class. Even over the last hundred years there have been times, such as 1906, 1945, and even the mid-1960s and 1970s, when the confidence of the Conservative Party has been sufficiently shaken for it to assume briefly a defeatist, oppositional mentality

It has been the remarkable capacity of the Conservative Party to adapt and survive which has enabled it to come back repeatedly from defeat, and re-establish its dominance. This perhaps suggests that the party has carried any ideological baggage lightly. There have been several noted occasions when the Conservative Party, in Disraeli's apt description, has caught its political opponents bathing and stolen their clothes. Even so, it might be doubted whether the British Conservative Party has been notably more adaptable than either the Liberal Party or, in its comparatively shorter history, the Labour Party.

But is not just its flexibility which makes conservatism a somewhat problematic ideology for systematic exploration. What is also noteworthy about British conservatism is its comparative intellectual poverty, an absence of great texts or authoritative statements of philosophy. Conservative ideology has to be substantially inferred from the actions of Conservative governments, from party programmes and the speeches and pronouncements of practising politicians. Such ideological inspiration which it has sought has often come from outside its own ranks – from the Whig Edmund Burke, from the radical Liberal Unionist Joseph Chamberlain, from Keynes, and more recently from classical liberalism and neo-liberalism. This seems to confirm the pragmatic nature of conservatism.

Even so, it will be argued here that conservatism is an ideology, at least in the sense outlined in the opening chapter. It will be further claimed that although there are considerable tensions within conservatism, in particular the rival libertarian and collectivist traditions of thought identified by Greenleaf (1973), there are, nevertheless, fairly consistent features of conservative ideology, some of which date back three centuries or more.

Indeed, despite the association of conservatism with pragmatism and flexible adaptation, paradoxically it is possible to argue that conservatism as a political ideology has not changed markedly over the years. The editor of one anthology of conservative thinking has commented, 'An impressive feature of all these expressions of Conservative beliefs is the consistency of outlook which runs from Halifax and Burke to Churchill and Lord Hugh Cecil' (Buck, 1975, p. 26). There is surely some truth in this. While there have been changes certainly in the presentation of conservatism, and more significant changes in policy and strategy, it can be argued that the basic conservative outlook has altered little (Blake, 1985, pp. 359–68). Whereas British liberalism has evolved and changed substantially over the last two centuries, conservatism is a much more static ideology. It is, then, possible to illustrate aspects of conservative thinking from quotations drawn almost indiscriminately across three or four centuries. This is one reason why the historical approach adopted for the examination of liberalism seems less appropriate for conservatism. There is not the same clear pattern of evolution and transformation against a changing historical background. Rather there is a continuity of themes over three or more centuries, and it is these themes which will here be explored.

The Tory tradition

Just as liberalism emerged out of the Whig tradition, conservatism grew out of the Tory tradition. This creates some additional complications in the case of conservatism, for while the term 'Whig' has dropped out of modern political discourse, 'Tory' is still a familiar synonym for Conservative. Here, we are essentially concerned with the Tory foundations of modern British conservatism. Historically, Toryism, like Whiggism, dates from the seventeenth century, while its antecedents can be traced back further, whereas Conservatism derives from Sir Robert Peel's modernisation of his party, and more specifically from the Tamworth Manifesto of 1835. Strictly, the label 'Conservative' should not be used before then; but just as the term 'liberalism' is often extended backwards in time to include earlier thinkers who would not have used or even known the word, so the conservative tradition is frequently and not unreasonably taken to encompass thinkers and ideas which seem to provide the foundations for the subsequent development of conservative ideology. In this context the rather unhistorical use of the term 'Conservative' rather than 'Tory' is useful in claiming for conservatism individuals like Edmund Burke, who was actually a Whig politician in his lifetime and could not be described as a Tory. Thus conservatism can be projected backwards before 1835 in a sense which distinguishes it from Toryism. Some writers would also project the term 'Tory' forwards after 1835, to denote the older, traditional ideas and interests within the conservative tradition, but this has never involved a clear-cut distinction with conservatism, rather a difference in emphasis. In common parlance a 'Tory' is not even a particular type of Conservative, but simply a Conservative.

There are some who would deny that modern conservatism has anything much to do with seventeenth- and eighteenth-century Toryism. It must also be admitted that the descriptions 'Whig' and 'Tory' were pretty loose, lacking in precision and variable over time. Even so, it is possible to make some reasonably valid generalisations on the values and interests associated with each political creed. While the Whigs wished to limit royal authority, the Tories supported the monarchy. The Whigs upheld the right to religious dissent, while the Tories were the party of the Church of England. Most important of all perhaps, the Whigs, although led by aristocratic landowners, were associated with developing commercial and manufacturing interests, while the Tories were the party of the landed gentry – small squires rather than great landowners. There are clearly some elements of continuity with the twentieth-century Conservative Party, for whom the crown and monarchy are still important symbols, which retains sufficient links with the Church of England to justify the latter's description as 'the Tory Party at prayer' despite recent friction between the party's leaders and some prominent clerics, and which still has ties of reciprocal dependence with the landed interest. Behind these interests the Tories stood for traditional authority and hierarchy in society, although such ideas were less systematically articulated than their Whig counterparts.

Reaction and gradualism

Tories and conservatives are often pejoratively described as re-actionaries. In fact the British right has rarely been reactionary in the sense of wishing to put the clock back to allow the restoration of some previous constitutional order or regime, although in the eighteenth century the Tory cause was for a time tainted with, and divided by, Jacobitism. Since then, British conservatism has not been weakened by divided loyalties to dispossessed regimes. This contrasts with the state of the right in countries like Italy and Spain, but above all, France under the Third Republic where the allegiance of the right was divided between two mutually hostile groups of monarchists, Bonapartists, supporters of opportunist adventurers like Boulanger, and, later, assorted quasi-fascist groups.

British Tories and conservatives might, however, be described as reactionary in the more literal sense of reacting against claims made by their opponents, as must any group of people whose interests are essentially bound up with the status quo. In the seventeenth century, for example, they were reacting against the Puritan assault on the authority of the Church in general and bishops in particular, against the limits the parliamentary opposition to the Stuarts wished to place on royal authority, and against new sources of income and wealth which appeared to threaten their interests.

Eighteenth-century Toryism and nineteenth-century conservatism can be seen more generally as a reaction against the major upheavals and developments in the western world over that period. Here, there is a clear contrast with liberalism. Liberalism was a product of the eighteenth-century Enlightenment, the American and French Revolutions, and, most important of all, of industrial capitalism. Toryism, and subsequently conservatism, involved a reaction against all these. It was suspicious of the claims made for reason by writers of the Enlightenment, and with the threat this presented to traditional secular and spiritual authority. It was hostile to the language of equal rights expressed by the American rebels and French revolutionaries, and particularly horrified by the claims and conduct of the latter. It was fearful of many of the changes resulting from industrialisation, and the ideas associated with it. Many Tory squires felt threatened by the new wealth and its growing political weight.

Edmund Burke (1729–97) played a leading role in the reaction against some of the major developments of his time, most notably the ideas associated with the Enlightenment and the French Revolution. However, in many ways he is a strange figure to be regarded as one of the founding fathers of British conservatism. He was Irish by birth, and for most of his life a prominent Whig politician, regarding himself as a Whig to his death. Like all Whigs he celebrated the Glorious Revolution of 1688. He also supported the Americans in their War of Independence, and was a leading and eloquent critic of George III's party.

What split Burke from his old Whig friends and associates was the French Revolution. Some Whigs, like Fox, greeted this with enthusiasm, and remained broadly sympathetic to it subsequently. Others initially viewed it favourably, and were afterwards disillusioned by the course it took, Burke was horrified from the start, and wrote his *Reflections on the French Revolution* in response (1790) (Hill, 1975). At the time this was regarded by his former colleagues as a betrayal of the principles he had formerly stood for. Burke himself was careful to distinguish what he regarded as the essentially conservative ideas behind the English revolution of 1688 from the more radical ideas behind the French Revolution:

> The very idea of the fabrication of a new government is enough to fill us with disgust and horror. We wished at the period of the Revolution [i.e. 1688] and do now wish, to derive all we possess as an inheritance from our forefathers. Upon that body and stock of inheritance we have taken care not to inoculate any scion alien to the nature of the original plant. All the reformations we have hitherto made have proceeded upon the principle of reference to antiquity; and I hope,

nay I am persuaded, that all those which possibly may be made here-
after will be carefully formed upon analogical precedent, authority
and example. (*Reflections on the French Revolution*, p. 296 of
collection of Burke's writing edited by Hill, 1975)

There is much which is significant for an understanding of conservative ideology here. In the plant metaphor there is an explicit
recognition of an organic theory of society and the state, which
contrasts markedly with the mechanistic and individualistic assumptions behind the Whig/liberal tradition. It is indeed this organic
conception of society that some commentators have seen as the very
essence of conservatism (Buck, 1975, p. 26). Burke also shows
a marked hostility to the liberal notion that social and political
institutions can be remodelled from first principles. There is reference to the importance of inheritance from the past, and reverence
for tradition and authority. There is a clear preference for gradualism over radical change. Reforms must be carefully grafted onto the
existing political and social system.

A preference for gradual reform, rather than reaction on the one
hand or radical change on the other, has often been seen as almost
a defining characteristic of British conservatism – although there are
some significant exceptions, including Disraeli, Joseph Chamberlain (if indeed he properly belongs to conservatism at all) and Mrs
Thatcher. What might be considered the mainstream gradualist
line is represented by the 'trimmer' Halifax from the seventeenth
century, Burke from the eighteenth, Sir Robert Peel from the
nineteenth and Michael Oakeshott from the twentieth.

Sir Robert Peel (1788–1850), the founder of the modern Conservative Party, might be considered the best exemplar of conservative
gradualism. On three major issues – Catholic Emancipation, Parliamentary Reform, and Corn Law Repeal – he long resisted change,
but finally conceded it. He helped Wellington carry Catholic Emancipation in 1829 once he became convinced it was necessary. He opposed parliamentary reform, but once the 1832 Reform Act was passed, recognised that the clock could not be put back in the Tamworth
Manifesto, which clearly articulated his own gradualist approach to
reform (Buck, 1975, pp. 56–8). Finally, after years of defending the
Corn Laws which protected British agriculture, he became convinced that their repeal was necessary, and carried it through with
Whig support against the majority of his own party in 1846.

Michael Oakeshott, an influential modern defender of conservatism, has written eloquently on what he calls the 'conservative disposition', and more particularly on the conservative attitude to change and innovation. 'To be conservative,' he suggests, 'is to prefer the known to the unknown, to prefer the tried to the untried, fact to mystery, the actual to the possible, the limited to the unbounded . . .'. Because the conservative enjoys the present he is generally averse to change. 'Consequently, he will find small and slow changes more tolerable than large and sudden; and he will value highly every appearance of continuity.' Proposed innovations should be assessed cautiously. 'Innovation entails certain loss and possible gain, therefore, the onus of proof . . . rests with the would-be innovator.' Innovations which appear to grow out of the present, which are in response to some specific defect, which are 'small and limited', and which are slow rather than rapid, should be preferred. 'The man of conservative temperament believes that a known good is not lightly to be surrendered for an unknown better.' (Oakeshott, 1962, pp. 168ff.)

Implicit behind such conservative caution in the face of demands for innovation and change is, of course, what critics might characterise as some fairly complacent assumptions about the present. Those less able to identify 'known goods' in their own circumstances, or in those of society in general, are more ready to embrace the risks involved in more radical change.

Suspicion of reason

Some commentators have argued that conservatism at bottom involves a relatively pessimistic view of human nature and human potential for individual improvement or social progress. It is a 'philosophy of imperfection' (O'Sullivan, 1976; Quinton, 1978). Compared with liberalism or socialism, less reliance is placed on the reason or the inherent goodness of man, and there is, accordingly, less optimism about the prospects for improving society. Consequently, more emphasis is placed on the importance of leadership, on respect for authority and established institutions, and on the need for a framework of discipline and order. Society needs defending from both internal and external threats. Radical schemes for social and political reform are viewed as inherently suspect and potentially destructive. Existing social arrangements and institutions have stood the test of time and should as far as possible be conserved.

It is not that conservatism is deliberately irrational, as, for example, fascism unashamedly is. Conservative thinkers emphasise rather the limitations of reason. In some, this reflects religious convictions. The Elizabethan divine, Hooker, criticised those who would erect their own individual judgement against the state or the Church. He was not here criticising reason in general. On the contrary, Hooker believed that human reason was the gift of God. But individual reason is not to be relied upon for certain truth, only 'probable resolutions', and to press private judgement against established authority is thus highly dangerous (Harrison, 1965, pp. 11–25; Quinton, 1978, pp. 23–9). The conservative implications of this attitude are fairly clear.

Others, such as the Scottish philosopher David Hume (1711–76), based their suspicions of the claims made for reason on a more general scepticism regarding human knowledge, behaviour and motivation. Certain knowledge of the world is not obtainable. Reason is not the chief inspiration of human behaviour, but rather the slave of the passions. Men act as they do from passion or habit or deference to authority. In this sense, Hume had a more sceptical view of human potential for rational thought and conduct than some of his intellectual contemporaries both in France and Britain. Unsurprisingly, this led him also to cautious conclusions in matters of politics and government. The established is to be preferred to the untried, and reform undertaken only with care and moderation (Quinton, 1978, pp. 45–51).

Once more, however, it is Edmund Burke who expresses the conservative approach to reason most trenchantly. Burke was not afraid to challenge head on the rationalist assumptions of his time. 'In this enlightened age I am bold enough to confess that we are generally men of untaught feelings.' He goes on to affirm:

> We are afraid to put men to live and trade each on his private stock of reason, because we suspect that the stock in each man is small, and that the individuals would do better to avail themselves of the general bank and capital of nations and of ages. (Hill, 1975, p. 354)

There could be no more explicit denial of the notion of enlightened self-interest which underpins so much liberal thought. Burke argues that men do not in practice act particularly rationally, and suggests that most men would be better advised not to rely on their reason. Provocatively he champions what he calls 'prejudice' against what he refers to as 'naked reason'. What he means by prejudice might perhaps be less pejoratively described as instinct or even conscience. Burke clearly has a conception of human nature which is far removed from the dispassionate rational calculator assumed by Jeremy Bentham, and it is Bentham who is the explicit target of Benjamin Disraeli in an extravagant diatribe against the Age of Reason in general, and the British utilitarians in particular:

In this country since the peace [i.e. since 1815] there has been an attempt to advocate a reconstruction of society on a purely rational basis. The principle of utility has been powerfully developed. . . . There has been an attempt to reconstruct society on a basis of material motives and calculations. It has failed. . . . How limited is human reason, the profoundest of enquirers are most conscious. We are not indebted to the reason of man for any of the great achievements which are the landmarks of human action and human progress. It was not reason which besieged Troy; it was not reason that sent forth the Saracen from the desert to conquer the world; that inspired the crusades; that instituted the monastic orders; it was not reason that produced the Jesuits; above all it was not reason that created the French Revolution. Man is only truly great when he acts from the passions; never irresistible but when he appeals to the imagination. Even Mormon counts more votaries than Bentham. (Disraeli, 1844, p. 262)

Disraeli's distrust of reason is characteristic of British conservatism, although he is rather untypical in not deriving cautious conclusions from his distrust; on the contrary he appears in this passage to embrace a distinct preference for the heroic over the humdrum and familiar. Perhaps there is an indication here of the psychology behind his later 'leap in the dark' over the Second Reform Act in 1867.

More typically conservative is Michael Oakeshott's attack on 'Rationalism in politics'. The Rationalist, says Oakeshott, 'stands for independence of mind on all occasions, for thought free from obligation to any authority save the authority of "reason".' He is 'the enemy of authority, of prejudice, of the merely traditional, customary or habitual'. This approach applied to politics means that 'to the Rationalist nothing is of value merely because it exists . . .

familiarity has no worth'. This means that he regards patching up and repair as a waste of time. 'He always prefers the invention of a new device to making use of a current and well-tried expedient.' Oakeshott goes on to suggest that rationalist politics are 'the politics of perfection' and 'the politics of uniformity'. Oakeshott is here attacking an outlook which is commonly associated with liberals or socialists. Voltaire, Godwin, Bentham, the Founding Fathers of the American Constitution, but most of all Marx and Engels, are castigated for applying a rationalist approach to politics, ultimately derived from what Oakeshott regards as the misguided search for certain knowledge by Bacon and Descartes. Oakeshott does not, however, specifically identify certain political creeds. Rather he seems to regard 'Rationalism' as a deplorable but almost all-pervasive outlook in modern politics. Even Hayek, who himself criticised the constructivist rationalism of such as Voltaire and Bentham, is singled out for censure. 'A plan to resist all planning may be better than its opposite, but it belongs to the same style of politics.' (Oakeshott, 1962, pp. 1–36)

Human nature

Some commentators would suggest that conservatism not only involves at least considerable reservations about individual intellectual capacities and the potential for rational conduct, but also implies some fairly pessimistic assumptions about human nature. Quintin Hogg has commented that 'man is an imperfect creature with a streak of evil as well as good in his inmost nature.' (Hogg, 1947, p. 11) Norman St John-Stevas has similarly observed that belief in the perfectability of man is a liberal or socialist error – conservatives have on the contrary a consciousness of original sin, although, Stevas goes on to point out, not everyone would give the point a theological formulation (St John-Stevas, 1982).

There is indeed a strong connection between conservative ideology and religious belief. The inherent weakness and wickedness of man has been proclaimed by Christian thinkers down the ages. Man is incapable of redeeming himself through his own efforts. Therefore, ideologies such as liberalism, socialism, and most especially anarchism, which present an optimistic picture of human nature and human potentiality, are at odds with mainstream orthodox

Christian faith, which suggests that Christ's intercession is necessary for human salvation. And, just as human beings are too inherently flawed to achieve everlasting salvation through their own unaided efforts, so these same weaknesses prevent spontaneous co-operative social endeavour, and require authority and strong government to keep men in order.

Anthony Quinton, while acknowledging the strength of the conservative religious tradition, has attempted to detach conservative doctrine 'from what is often alleged to be an essential dependence on religious foundations'. He distinguishes between a religious and secular tradition of conservative thought. One tradition, he argues, 'derives its conservative politics to some extent from religious premises, in particular from the moral imperfection of human nature.' Quinton associates Hooker, Clarendon, Johnson, Burke, Coleridge and Newman with this tradition. But Quinton also argues there is a 'secular tradition of conservative thinking' initiated by Halifax, Bolingbroke and Hume, and kept alive more recently by Oakeshott. This emphasises the 'radical intellectual imperfection of the human individual' as well as a 'parallel belief in the moral imperfection of mankind'. But Quinton considers that the latter, although sometimes derived from 'the Christian dogma of original sin', is also shared by many 'secular and even atheistic thinkers, for example Hobbes, Hume and Freud'. (Quinton, 1978, pp. 9–16)

It is perhaps unfortunate from Quinton's point of view that he is unable to claim Hobbes for this conservative secular tradition, for it was indeed Thomas Hobbes who painted one of the most celebrated and gloomy pictures of human nature in the raw. Without a common power to keep men in order there would be continuous war of every man against every man, and life would be 'solitary, poor, nasty, brutish and short'. It was this nightmare vision which required strong government, for Hobbes a government with absolute powers. But although Hobbes's general pessimism about human nature has been widely shared by conservative thinkers, he has been rarely claimed for British conservatism. Quinton disqualifies him on three counts – his absolutism, his rationalism, and his individualism (Quinton, 1978, p. 30).

Without Hobbes, Quinton's conservative secular tradition seems relatively insubstantial compared with what must be considered the mainstream Christian tradition. Many conservatives have quite explicitly associated their political principles with their Christian faith. Although there are liberals like Gladstone, and socialists like Tawney who have claimed to derive their political ideas from their Christianity, the association of these ideologies with Christianity is much less strong and explicit. To an extent Christianity, and more particularly Anglicanism, is highly compatible with conservatism. Not only do they share the same pessimistic assumptions about human nature, they also both involve an acceptance of authority and hierarchy, which might seem a logical corollary of human moral and intellectual deficiencies.

Authority, leadership, and Tory democracy

If individual human beings are not rational calculators, and if the general benevolence of most men and women is at least a doubtful question, then certain implications may be considered to follow. In particular, democracy appears a hazardous enterprise, and the hopes of nineteenth-century liberals like Mill that it could be indefinitely improved through education, naive.

In practice, the conservative has only partially embraced democracy, tempering an acceptance of representative institutions with a strong emphasis on leadership and authority. Earlier, democracy had been viewed with abhorrence. Peel opposed the first Reform Bill, objecting that 'all its tendencies are, to substitute for a mixed form of government, a pure unmitigated democracy' (debate on third reading, quoted in Wright, 1970, p. 119). Salisbury in 1860, reacting to demands for a further extension of the franchise, in similar vein referred to 'the struggle between the English constitution on the one hand, and the democratic forces which are now labouring to subvert it'. He argued that 'Wherever democracy has prevailed, the power of the State has been used in some form or other to plunder the well-to-do classes for the benefit of the poor' (Buck, 1975, p. 104).

Conservatives only moved to a qualified acceptance of democracy when it became clear that it was compatible with maintenance of the existing social order and the defence of property. Thus Disraeli perceived that the working classes could be won for Conservatism, and persuaded his party to 'dish the Whigs' by promoting the 1867 Reform Bill (Mackenzie and Silver, 1968). His judgement ed defective in the short run, for Gladstone's Liberals gained an emphatic victory in the ensuing 1868 election, but was vindicated in the longer run, as the Conservatives managed to win and subsequently hold a substantial minority of the working-class vote. Disraeli had earlier toyed with the idea of an alliance between the working classes and the aristocracy against the industrial bourgeoisie. Behind this rather fanciful notion there was a realisation that there was no harmony of interest between industrial workers and their liberal bosses. It was perhaps no accident that Lancashire, the home of 'Manchester liberalism', established a strong tradition of working-class conservatism.

Acceptance of democracy did not mean any real dilution of the characteristically conservative endorsement of authority, hierarchy, and the mixed constitution. Beer argues that 'Authoritative leadership is a permanent social necessity for the Tory.' He goes on to suggest that 'parliamentary government and the mass suffrage have been grafted onto and adapted to' a Tory view of the Constitution in which all the initiative comes from government. 'Tory democracy gives the voters power. But it is the power of control, not initiation, exercised under government by consent, not by delegation.' (Beer, 1982, pp. 94–8). This is very similar to the version of democracy later endorsed by Joseph Schumpeter (1943), in which all the initiative comes from leaders, rather than the masses. Democracy involves a constrained competition for the people's vote rather than popular participation in government.

Coupled with all this is the Tory view of an organic society composed of unequal but mutually dependent classes and groups, in which a relatively small group have the attributes, experience, and leisure to be qualified to govern. The mass of the people, in this view, are willing to defer to the judgement and experience of this governing class. Bagehot (1826–77) (himself a Liberal) suggested that the 'deference' of the English people was one of the main supports of the English Constitution. Lord Randolph Churchill (1849–95), who coined the term 'Tory democracy', believed it was possible to secure popular support for existing institutions. 'To rally the people round the Throne, and a patriotic people, that is our policy, and that is our faith.' (Buck, 1975, p. 102). The assumption is that there is a common national interest which transcends individual or class interests, that all to some degree share the benefits of an ordered society and system of government, that the poorest can be made to appreciate the sanctity of property and existing social arrangements.

To critics of conservatism this is a transparent confidence trick which serves to conceal from subordinate classes their own interests in sweeping reform or revolution. The Tory perspective can thus be summed up in the familiar couplet, 'God bless the squire and his relations, And keep us in our proper stations.' Conservatives would tend to respond that inequality is both natural and inevitable. To preach equality and social justice is to stir up envy, hatred, and unhappiness, for the passions aroused can never be satisfied. Moreover, the conservative would argue, everyone, ultimately, has an interest in the sanctity of property.

The defence of property

Conservatives have generally been unequivocal in their defence of property (Nisbet, 1986, pp. 55ff.), an attitude which contrasts strongly not only with that of socialists, but also liberals whose approach to the subject has been ambivalent. Starting from libertarian and egalitarian assumptions, a faith in reason and a distrust of traditional social arrangements, liberals have felt a need to produce elaborate justifications for property, based for example on natural rights, labour, or utility. Sometimes this has led them to justify some forms of property, but not others – there have been particular problems with land and inherited wealth. Conservatives have generally devoted less time and space to the justification of private property, for the simple reason that the issue for them is unproblematic. Existing property rights are part of traditional social arrangements endorsed by conservatives. Inequality in property reflects profound inequalities in abilities and energies. The conservative would concede that the existing distribution of property does not necessarily accord with desert, but would see this as an inevitable consequence of imperfect human social arrangements. Social justice is unobtainable, and attempts to justify interference with existing property rights in the name of social justice threaten the whole institution of private property. The most the conservative is generally prepared to concede is that the possession of property entails obligations and responsibilities.

Accordingly, conservatives have wholeheartedly defended private property, and justified its extremely unequal distribution. Burke argued that 'the characteristic essence of property, formed out of the combined principles of its acquisition and conservation, is to be unequal.' Great concentrations of property 'form a natural rampart about the lesser properties in all their gradations.' Inherited property is also strongly defended. 'The power of perpetuating our property in our families is one of the most valuable and interesting circumstances belonging to it, and that which tends the most to the perpetuation of society itself.' (Hill, 1975, pp. 316–17) Oakeshott associates the possession of private property with freedom, and goes on to suggest that private ownership of the means of production, essentially capitalism, is also necessary for liberty. 'The freedom which separates a man from slavery is nothing but a freedom to choose and to move among autonomous, independent organizations, firms, purchasers of labour, and this implies private property in resources other than personal capacity.' (Oakeshott, 1962, p. 46) Scruton (1980, p. 99) talks of 'man's absolute and ineradicable need of private property'. This, he says, 'represents the common intuition of every labouring person.' Against the classical liberal or the modern neo-liberal, Scruton is prepared to justify state regulation of private property and market forces, but at the same time he strongly attacks deliberate state intervention to achieve the redistribution of property through progressive taxation, wealth and inheritance taxes (Scruton, 1980, p. 108).

The problem with property for conservatives has been more one of strategy rather than of principle – how to persuade the majority with little or no property to accept the existing distribution of property. Conservatism was initially associated with a particular form of property – land, and indeed there still lingers among some conservatives a distrust of other forms of wealth (Nisbet, 1986, p. 63). Towards the end of the nineteenth century the British Conservative Party became the party, not just of landed property, but of property in general, as the manufacturing interest increasingly deserted the Liberals, alienated by radicalism and Irish Home Rule. However, a wider base of popular support was required for electoral survival.

Various strategies were employed in practice, including social reform and imperialism, but there has also been, particularly recently, a deliberate attempt to widen and extend property ownership. It was Eden who used the phrase 'property owning democracy' and post-war governments in particular have sought to promote home ownership, and, more recently, wider share ownership. Earlier, conservatives at both central and local level had supported public housing, and had been content to encourage home ownership through tax relief. In recent years, the party has encouraged and subsequently compelled the sale of council houses, and actively discouraged further council house building. The result has been to turn owner occupation into the majority form of housing tenure. Some tax concessions, but more notably the privatisation of major nationalised industries on favourable terms for small investors, has enabled Mrs Thatcher to claim that there are now more share owners than trade unionists. In this manner, the ownership of property, both in the tangible sense of bricks and mortar, and in the more symbolic participation in capitalism, has been significantly extended, although its uneven distribution remains substantially unchanged.

Paternalism and collectivism

Until perhaps recently, the defence of private property has not generally for conservatives entailed an unqualified defence also of the free market. It might indeed appear that 'self-help' and '*laissez-faire*' were inappropriate injunctions for the many people who, according to conservative views of human nature and intellectual capacity, were on the whole incapable of perceiving their own rational self-interest, and could not be relied upon to be particularly enlightened to its pursuit. On the contrary, it seemed clear to many Tories that such people needed help and guidance, and sometimes also firm control. The authority of the state was therefore required to provide a framework of order and discipline, but also support for those unable or incapable of helping themselves. Others who were fortunately placed in terms of natural endowments or wealth had an obligation to provide that help, guidance and control. Society was more than a mere aggregate of individuals. It was rather an organic whole, necessarily involving ties of mutual dependence, which in turn suggested social duties and responsibilities as well as individual rights. This was the basis for what has been termed 'Tory paternalism'.

Disraeli is the Conservative pre-eminently associated with paternalism. In his novel *Sybil* there is a strong attack, not only on the 1832

Reform Act, but also, and more importantly, on the whole system of capitalist values which Disraeli associated with industrialisation:

> If a spirit of rapacious covetousness, desecrating all the humanities of life, has been the besetting sin of England for the last century and a half, since the passing of the Reform Act the altar of Mammon has blazed with triple worship. To acquire, to accumulate, to plunder each other by virtue of philosophic phrases, to propose an Utopia to consist only of WEALTH and TOIL, this has been the breathless business of enfranchised England for the last twelve years. (Disraeli, 1845, p. 56)

Here Disraeli is assaulting all the ideas and slogans associated with the Whig/liberal tradition of thought, but particularly those of *laissez-faire* economics. Behind such wholesale condemnations of new values and interests lay a nostalgia for a vanished past which perhaps only existed in Disraeli's romantic imagination – an ordered society of mutual dependence, where privilege entailed obligations to those less fortunate and where social divisions and class conflict did not exist. For Disraeli liked to think that somehow social conflict could be healed. In another often quoted passage from *Sybil* he talks of the Victorian England of his day in terms of two nations of the rich and the poor.

> Two nations; between whom there is no intercourse and no sympathy; who are as ignorant of each other's habits, thoughts and feelings, as if they were dwellers in different zones, or inhabitants of different planets; who are formed by different breeding, are fed by different food, are ordered by different manners, and are not governed by the same laws. (Disraeli, 1845, p. 96)

Disraeli was fully aware of the depth of social divisions in the England of his day, but like later Conservatives who adopted the 'one nation' slogan, hoped that somehow they could be transcended and one nation made of two.

The Conservative Party has always claimed to stand above class and for the nation as a whole. For political opponents, particularly for socialists, this is a transparent 'con trick' – a capitalist society necessarily involves class conflict, and conservatives mask this social reality in their own interests (Honderich, 1990, chs 6, 7). And Disraeli himself sometimes reveals an element of class interest in his concern for social reform; for example, in a comment in 1848 'the palace is not safe, when the cottage is not happy' (quoted in Beer, 1982, p. 267). Even so, Conservative politicians have had little difficulty in convincing themselves of the idea of a conservatism standing for the nation and against sectional interests, and it has had a potent appeal.

It should be noted, however, that this paternalism did not then necessarily imply state action. Disraeli's biographer has claimed, 'He had a genuine hatred of centralization, bureaucracy and every manifestation of the Benthamite state.' (Blake, 1966, p. 282) For Disraeli the state was almost the last rather than the first resort. He was well aware that for numbers of the poor 'self-help' was a futile injunction, but anticipated that the help they required should be forthcoming from the traditional aristocracy, from the church, and from voluntary activity of all kinds. In *Sybil* his targets were the uncaring landowners who neglected their tenants and the new capitalists who exploited their workforce, and these are contrasted with examples of philanthropic aristocrats and caring industrialists. In his political speeches he took much the same line. At Shrewsbury in 1843 he blamed current political evils on the development of property divorced from duty (Eccleshall, 1990, p. 116). Much of this, of course, runs directly counter to the notion of rational self-interest and self-help, but hardly suggests that Disraeli saw the state as the principal vehicle for the alleviation of social distress.

Arguably, he became more committed to state action subsequently. In his 1872 speech to the National Union he described the 'elevation of the condition of the people' as the third great object of the Tory Party, although the speech was longer on rhetoric than specifics. While much has been made of Disraeli's commitment to social reform, both before and after he became prime minister (Beer, 1982, ch. 9), recent historians have exposed the myth that there was any clear consistent programme of social reform behind his administration's legislative record (Smith, 1967, p. 202). Disraeli's modern biographer, Lord Blake, apparently anxious to re-establish his subject's conservative credentials in a Thatcherite era, has observed, 'His policies have been much misinterpreted, not least by those who unplausibly regard him as an ancestor of the welfare state – a sort of arch wet.' (*The Guardian*, 4 October 1982)

The commitment of Disraeli's immediate successors to social reform is still more questionable. Randolph Churchill's enthusiasm for Tory democracy and reform involved more rhetoric than solid reality, but his early resignation in any case removed any prospect that Salisbury's government would pursue the social question. Even the adhesion of the radical Liberal Unionist, Joseph Chamberlain, made little difference to what has been described as a period of 'Conservative inertia.' (Beer, 1982, p. 271) Indeed, by 1894 Chamberlain had so far moderated his earlier radicalism to complain that 'the resolutions of the TUC . . . amount to universal confiscation in order to create a Collectivisit State.' (quoted in Adelman, 1970, p. 107)

Protection and Tory collectivism

In so far as some Conservatives wished to interfere with market forces, it was less in the interests of social reform than economic protection and industrial reorganisation. The demand for 'fair trade' as opposed to 'free trade' was articulated on the Tory benches in the late nineteenth century. Joseph Chamberlain turned the issue into a veritable crusade with his demand for imperial protection. It was this issue on which Baldwin's 1923 government was defeated at the polls, and it was the Conservative protectionists whose views eventually prevailed in the National government of the 1930s. Neville Chamberlain as Chancellor of the Exchequer was to boast that his Import Duties Bill provided the government with 'a lever as has never been possessed before by any government for inducing or, if you like, forcing industry to set its house in order.' (quoted in Beer, 1982, p. 293)

It is perhaps worth observing here that there has been some confusion of the terms 'paternalism', 'collectivism' and 'socialism'. It has been noted already that paternalism need not involve state action. Nor, despite their association in modern Thatcherist rhetoric, is collectivism to be necessarily identified with socialism, a point which Gilmour emphasises when he carefully describes Chamberlain's policies as 'collectivist . . . rather than socialist' (Gilmour, 1978, p. 36). Interventionist policies to rationalise industry of the kind pursued by the National government of the 1930s involved managed capitalism rather than socialism. It should be conceded, however, that Neville Chamberlain did also have a respectable record as a social reformer, particularly in the housing field.

But it was the post-war conservatism which can be most plausibly associated with collectivism. Macmillan had once provocatively declared that Toryism had always been a kind of paternal socialism. He preached an interventionist 'middle way' between *laissez-faire* capitalism and socialist state planning (Eccleshall, 1990, p. 192). The wartime Tory Reform Group urged the acceptance of social reform, and more specifically the Beveridge Report which was declared the 'very essence of Toryism' (quoted in Beer, 1982, p. 307). In opposition the commitment to social reform was firmed up. Butler, the architect of the 1944 Education Act, declared in 1947 'We are not frightened at the use of the State. A good Tory has never in history been afraid of the use of the State.' This sweeping and surely inaccurate verdict was endorsed by Anthony Eden. 'We are not the political children of the *laissez-faire* school. We opposed them decade after decade.' (quoted in Beer, 1982, p. 271)

The rhetoric of these modern-day heirs of Disraeli was rather more matched by reality than that of the great Victorian politician. The Welfare state established by the coalition and Labour governments was maintained, and even in certain respects enhanced. A policy of compromise and accommodation was applied to labour and the trade unions. Most remarkably perhaps, after the initial denationalisation of steel and road haulage, other state-owned industries were maintained. Overall, the role of government continued to expand, and public expenditure continued to rise. Macmillan accepted the resignation of his entire Treasury team in 1958 rather than the cuts in spending which they demanded. The commitment to full employment policies was maintained, through orthodox Keynesian demand management policies, by successive Tory chancellors. When such policies did not succeed in correcting such deep-seated problems as low growth, balance of payments deficits, and weak sterling, Macmillan's government moved towards more intervention rather than free market solutions. The National Economic Development Council signalled a new interest in long-term economic planning, and the National Incomes Commission institutionalised the new Conservative concern with incomes policy. This was perhaps the high-water mark of Tory collectivism.

As with liberal critics of the New Liberalism, there are some conservatives who would regard this whole approach as a monstrous aberration, a departure from true conservatism. A few who participated in these governments, such as, most notably, Lord Joseph (1976), have since recanted, and declared they only discovered true conservatism subsequently. Others, such as Sir Ian Gilmour (1978), have continued to claim that Butler and Macmillan represent the mainstream Tory tradition, and that it is the free market neo-liberal nostrums of the New Right which are heretical. There are, indeed, some interpretations of conservatism, particularly S. H. Beer's (1982), which have seen the post-war 'one nation' Conservatism as the culmination of a Tory collectivist tradition, but this has always involved a rather selective interpretation of Conservative history. Beer emphasises some periods and some individuals, and ignores others. Salisbury (Conservative Party leader 1885–1902) presided over Conservative Party fortunes longer than Disraeli, and has some claims to be considered an important conservative thinker, but is not even mentioned by Beer, who dismisses his period of dominance as a period of 'Conservative inertia'. Rather more convincing is Greenleaf's (1973) portrayal of a continuing tension within conservatism between its libertarian and collectivist strands. Greenleaf regards both strands as part of an authentic conservative tradition.

Arguably, however, both the libertarian and collectivist strands of conservatism require a strong state and an emphasis on leadership and authority, which would be anathema to many liberals and socialists (Gamble, 1988). The need for leadership has been a perennial Tory theme, from Bolingbroke in the eighteenth century, through Carlyle and Disraeli in the nineteenth century, to Churchill and Mrs Thatcher in the twentieth century. Respect for authority is a key message in the thought of Burke and Salisbury. The free economy advocated by the modern New Right is widely perceived as requiring a strong state. Government might abdicate some of its functions, but not its power and authority. Government indeed has to be strong to provide the conditions for the market to operate. It has to be strong to resist pressures and claims upon it from powerful sectional interests including both producer and consumer groups.

Patriotism and imperialism

Reverence for the authority of the state chimed in easily with conservative nationalism and imperialism. Yet until the later nineteenth century, conservatism had no monopoly of patriotic sentiment. Nationalism was closely associated with liberalism, and the

Whig–Liberal prime minister Palmerston had been notably successful in exploiting patriotic feeling in his own and his party's interest.
By the end of the century, however, Gladstone's Irish policy and his
internationalism, and subsequent Liberal divisions over the Boer
War, coupled with Disraeli's assiduous promotion of imperialism
and the national interest, associated conservatism with patriotism.
This proved a highly successful electoral strategy, particularly with
the newly enfranchised working classes. Beer observes, 'In imperialism . . . the party had found a cause with a mighty appeal to the
voter.' He goes on to note that 'only from the election of 1886 . . .
did the party win those majorities of the popular vote which eluded
even Disraeli' and concludes that imperialism had made Tory social
reform redundant (Beer, 1982, p. 272).

McKenzie and Silver (1968) clearly document Conservative Party
literature addressed to the electorate which exploited nationalist
and imperialist sentiment from the 1880s to the 1960s. Liberals,
radicals and socialists were constantly accused of being unpatriotic
and undermining English and imperial interests. The Liberal government in 1895 was accused of being 'a weak, vacillating, craven
Ministry . . . which dares not defend British interests effectively,
and which will submit to be kicked and kicked and kicked until at
last the spirit of the English people is aroused in its majesty' (quoted
in McKenzie and Silver, 1968, p. 53). In 1900 the radicals were
associated with 'a Small England, a Shrunken England, a Degraded
England, a Submissive England' (p. 56). By 1910 socialists were
associated with radicals in a Conservative pamphlet which claimed
'If you fight for radical socialism you fight for a divided nation . . . a
divided Kingdom – the union sold! a British Isle no more, Ireland
breeds treason at the Empire's core' (pp. 63–4). In 1924 the Labour
government was accused of putting 'the foreigner first' and prefer-
ring 'the Bolsheviks to our own people' (p. 65). In 1951 it was
argued 'Socialists sneered and still sneer at what they call "Imperialism". . . . The Conservative Party, by long tradition and settled
belief, is the Party of the Empire' (p. 68).

While such language is not found in more erudite statements of
party philosophy, it could be argued that it is perhaps a better guide
to the popular appeal and interpretation of conservatism. Of course,
nationalist sentiment is by no means confined to the Conservative
Party. The music halls, the press, and later the electronic media
have helped create a popular nationalist culture which has also

coloured British liberalism and labourism (Schwarz, in Donald and Hall, 1986, p. 177). But it was the Conservative Party which most successfully exploited the patriotic theme, reinforcing claims to stand above narrow class interests and for the nation as a whole. 'Being Conservative is only another way of being British' claimed Quinton Hogg (quoted by McKenzie and Silver, 1968, p. 18).

Baldwin and Churchill in their different ways were particularly skilful in associating themselves and their party with British values and interests. The more internationalist climate in the post-Second World War era, coupled with the decline in the British empire and British power, for a time made patriotic rhetoric appear somewhat outmoded. Under Macmillan and then Heath the Conservatives pursued entry into the European Community, and appeared to have converted their party to the European ideal. However, Enoch Powell's English nationalism, expressed in his opposition to black immigration, the EC, and concessions to the opposition in Ulster, although scorned by the establishment and rejected by Heath, showed that chauvinism still had popular appeal, not least from elements of the working class. This has been further demonstrated by Mrs Thatcher. While the Falklands has been the most dramatic illustration of this renewed conservative nationalism, the emphatic assertion of British interests has been a consistent theme in defence and foreign policy since 1979.

Conservatism and Thatcherism

No examination of British conservatism would be complete without some discussion of what has come to be called 'Thatcherism'. Unlike socialism or even liberalism, British conservatism has not previously been much concerned with doctrinal disputes. Such disputes as have occurred within conservatism have been more tactical than theoretical. Indeed, as has been noticed, ideas have not been systematically elaborated. Conservatism has evolved as a broad church, with, inevitably, some internal tensions, but with little in the way of doctrinal purity to advance and defend. There is nothing remotely resembling Labour's celebrated 'clause four', for example, to serve as an article of conservative faith. There have been no major doctrinal splits, and few, if any, allegations of heresy.

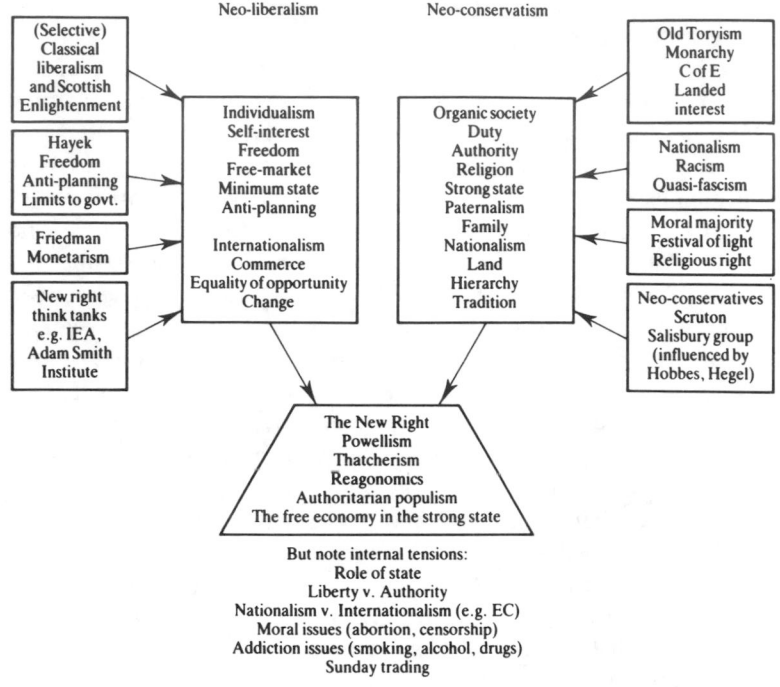

Figure 4.1   The New Right and Thatcherism

Arguably, this is no longer true. Both conservatives and their critics have suggested that Mrs Thatcher's leadership entailed a sharp break with the mainstream Tory tradition. Some have even alleged that her brand of conservatism has more in common with nineteenth-century liberalism, historically the antithesis of Toryism. In this context, Milton Friedman has claimed 'Margaret Thatcher is not in terms of beliefs a Tory. She is a nineteenth-century Liberal' (*Observer*, 26 September 1982). This perception was shared by at least one of Mrs Thatcher's leading supporters and admirers, her first defence secretary, John Nott. It is also given some substance by Mrs Thatcher's own early speeches as leader of the Opposition, where she extolled Victorian virtues of self-reliance, attacked collectivism, and dismissively referred to 'bourgeois guilt', a phrase widely interpreted as a criticism of Tory paternalism as much as socialism. She also acknowledged the influence of two celebrated neo-liberals, Friedman and Hayek, and, behind them, the virtual founder of classical economics, Adam Smith (Thatcher, 1977). Even while Mrs Thatcher was still in opposition, the liberal rhetoric disturbed both critics and some admirers within the Conservative Party. Sir Ian Gilmour, later to become a victim of one of Mrs Thatcher's first cabinet sackings, carefully distinguished between Conservatism and Liberalism in his book *Inside Right* (1978). William Waldegrave (1978), a later recruit into Thatcher's government, attacked neo-liberalism, and reasserted a Conservative tradition involving the acceptance of state power. Several contributors to a generally sympathetic volume of *Conservative Essays* edited by Maurice Cowling (1978) were expressly critical of liberal ideas. Peregrine Worsthorne referred dismissively to 'Some libertarian mishmash drawn from the writings of Adam Smith, John Stuart Mill, and the warmed up milk of nineteenth-century liberalism' (Cowling, 1978, p. 149). Roger Scruton, another contributor, went on to produce his own elucidation of conservatism, in which liberalism was subjected to rather more scornful criticism than Marxism (Scruton, 1980).

The post-Thatcher divisions within the Conservative Party were early popularised as a distinction between 'Wets' and 'Drys', which does not necessarily equate with a distinction between conservatism and liberalism. In so far as the labels relate to theory rather than style, the 'Drys' were associated with fashionable monetarist ideas, the 'Wets' with the apparently discredited Keynesianism (Keegan, 1984). 'Monetarism' was never a very helpful label to describe the new conservative ideas, however. Monetarist policies were initiated by the previous Labour government, and were not distinctively Thatcherite. Moreover, it soon became clear that there were fundamental problems in attempting to control the money supply, and subsequently the Thatcher government quietly abandoned monetarism.

The term 'monetarism' to describe the approach of the new government soon gave way to the lables 'Thatcherism', and the 'New Right'. Neither label is ideal. 'Thatcherism' perhaps over-personalises the developments in ideas which have taken place, and may say more about policy making style than content. 'The New Right' has a broader, international connotation, but this raises further problems of definition and interpretation.

The radical and Marxist left have provided an influential analysis of Thatcherism, which is seen as combining some traditional conservative elements – patriotism, law and order, authority and strong government – summed up by the term 'authoritarian populism', coupled with free market economics (Hall and Jacques, 1983; Edgar, 1984; Gamble, 1988). Most British-oriented texts on the New Right have emphasised the latter, and have presented the phenomenon largely in terms of economic theory (Bosanquet, 1983; Green, 1987). A broader, international perspective suggests a distinction between neo-liberalism and neo-conservatism (Levitas, 1986). Both involve a reaction against what have been perceived as dominant orthodoxies of the recent past. Neo-liberalism is a reaction against Keynesianism and the Welfare State. Neo-conservatism involves a traditionalist reaction against progressive liberal permissiveness. To an extent, both are combined in Thatcherism, as the radical Marxist analysis suggests, and to a degree the two strands of thought are compatible. Both suggest hostility to trade unionism, bureaucracy, and corporatist tendencies in government. Nevertheless, there are also tensions – on foreign policy and Europe, where neo-conservatives seek to protect national sovereignty and interests – on the environment, where neo-conservatives tend to be right-wing conservationists, while neo-liberals seek to remove controls on planning and development – on a host of moral issues, such as abortion, censorship, and Sunday trading.

The record of the Thatcher governments (Riddell, 1983; Young, 1989) shows strong elements of both neo-liberal and neo-conservative thinking. The massive privatisation programme, the introduction of compulsory competitive tendering and deregulation, the legislation on trade unions, and the changes introduced or threatened in the universities, the legal profession and the medical profession, all reflect the influence of neo-liberal economics. By contrast, the Falklands War, Mrs Thatcher's approach to Europe, firm controls on immigration, tough penal policies, and the National Curriculum in education are hardly inspired by free market ideas, and are more in keeping with traditional conservatism.

The extent of the ideological shift can be exaggerated, however. The traditional authoritarian streak in Thatcherism may involve a break from the liberal progressive attitudes of Macmillan, Butler, Macleod, Boyle and Heath, but reflects the attitudes and demands which have regularly surfaced from the rank and file at

Conservative Party conferences throughout the post-war period. Also, the libertarian strand in conservatism is not new, as Greenleaf (1973) has demonstrated. Even in the supposed heyday of Tory collectivism there were strong pressures for competition. The Conservatives were re-elected to the slogan 'Set the People Free' in 1951, and proceeded to dismantle rationing and controls, denationalise steel and road haulage, establish commercial television and, later, commercial radio, relax rent controls, and abolish resale price maintenance. Even the sale of council houses, sometimes regarded as quintessential Thatcherism, was Conservative policy in the 1950s. Mrs Thatcher's government was responsible for their forced sale at substantial discounts. Both that and the privatisation of assets at below their market value indicate a greater interest in the political success of policies than their economic rationale.

This suggests a substantial element of traditional conservative pragmatism. Indeed, it can be argued that it is circumstances rather than the ideology of the Conservative Party which has changed. In the post-war period it seemed that commitment to the Welfare State and full employment was necessary to win elections. More recently, both the economic assumptions behind those commitments and their political rationale were seen as questionable. Faith in Keynesian demand management was undermined by the performance of the economy in the 1970s, and a growing proportion of the electorate seemed disillusioned with both the benefits of the Welfare State and its mounting cost, with adverse consequences for taxation and take-home pay. Thatcherism thus involved a response to the new mood. It can be seen in terms of the politics of statecraft, the construction of new coalitions of interests (Bulpitt, 1987). Mrs Thatcher, like Disraeli over a century before, was making a bid for the skilled working-class vote.

There is clearly something in such analysis, although in her third term Mrs Thatcher's government pursued policies which seem to have a clearer ideological than electoral rationale. The changes in local government finance, the reform of the health service, the privatisation of water, and the almost exclusive reliance on high interest rates to combat inflation seem to owe more to neo-liberal economic theory, than to any electoral calculations. At the same time perhaps the aspect of all this which runs counter to traditional conservatism is not so much the neo-liberal economics, as the pace of change. However Thatcherism is defined, it cannot be equated with gradualism. There are few precedents in Britain for Mrs Thatcher's brand of right-wing radicalism.

Prospects for conservatism

The long-term future direction of conservative ideology in Britain is an open question. It is not clear yet how far Thatcherism can survive without Mrs Thatcher, but a strong reaction in the Conservative Party against the policies pursued since 1979 seems unlikely. Too many leading Conservatives have been implicated in Thatcherism to make total repudiation a credible option.

But some reaction against the pace of change of recent years, and a return to more traditional conservative gradualism, does seem possible. There has been increasing pressure for consolidation and caution. Beyond that, a more pragmatic attitude to economic intervention is likely. Environmentalist considerations, already acknowledged by Mrs Thatcher, reinforced in some parts of the country by electoral calculations, will provide strong pressures for interference with market forces. Professional groups like lawyers and doctors and the agricultural lobby may see some of their former influence restored. Corporatist arrangements may enjoy a return to fashion.

When Thatcherism is seen in perspective, it may appear as neither an aberration nor a transformation in British conservatism, but a period which is generally consistent with the broad Tory tradition, although showing a few unusual features. Inevitably, there will be some reassessment of Mrs Thatcher's government, and the governments of her predecessors, and this itself will subtly influence the future development of conservatism, which, in the absence of any doctrinal purity has always set considerable store on past leaders as role models.

5

Labourism and Socialism

Perspectives on socialism

The nature and definition of socialism is far more problematic and controversial than that of conservatism or liberalism. Differences over the interpretation of conservatism tend to revolve around questions of emphasis rather than fundamentals. Within liberalism, differences have been deeper, particularly relating to the legitimacy or otherwise of the New Liberalism. The debate over socialism involves far more fundamental divisions. Many of those who regard themselves as socialists would vehemently deny the claims of others to the same description. Some of the differences are over values and objectives, others over the means of achieving socialism.

Many of these differences are found in debates on socialism the world over. Yet there are features peculiar to the nature and development of socialism in Britain. Some strands of thought which were strong in other countries, such as Marxism and anarcho-syndicalism, have been relatively weak in Britain. By contrast, the main elements of what was termed 'revisionism' among socialists abroad were established so early in Britain as to make the term 'revisionist' rather inappropriate. Quite simply, there was little fundamentalist socialism in Britain to revise. Indeed, it is an open question whether 'socialism' is the most appropriate label for describing the mainstream ideas associated with the British Labour Party, and some would prefer to use the term 'labourism'. Even so, the Labour Party has continued to contain socialists, and those socialists who have remained outside its ranks have (to echo a gibe by Nye Bevan to Jennie Lee) retained their purity at the cost of impotence. There is in Britain no significant left-wing or socialist rival to Labour. In many other countries different strands of left or socialist thought are represented in contending political parties. In Britain some of those strands are scarcely represented at all, while others are largely contained within the Labour Party.

Although socialism is the most international of political ideologies, British socialism is almost *sui generis* – of its own kind. Even at the elite level, there is a parochial flavour to much British socialist thought. It is British thinkers, such as Robert Owen, William Morris, the Webbs, R. H. Tawney, G. D. H. Cole, George Orwell and Anthony Crosland, who are cited as significant influences. This is still more evident at the popular level. The British Labour Party, the Labour movement and associated labour and socialist institutions, developed in their own highly individual ways. But in spite of this, it is still useful for purposes of explanation and critical evaluation to set British socialism and labourism within the context of a wider debate on socialist values and strategies.

Industrial capitalism and socialism

While precursors have been identified in earlier periods (Eccleshall *et al.*, 1984, pp. 119ff.), socialism only developed as a coherent ideology in the early nineteenth century. Essentially, socialism involved a reaction against, and a radical alternative to, industrial capitalism. If political ideologies can be linked with class interests, socialism can be seen as the political ideology of the new urban working class, effectively created by industrialisation, just as conservatism was, initially, the ideology of the landed interest and liberalism the ideology of the bourgeoisie, or manufacturing interest.

While conservatism involved a defence of the status quo or a return to the recent past, and liberalism provided a justification and support for an ongoing industrial transformation, socialism developed as a radical or revolutionary ideology requiring a fundamental transformation of existing society, and its underlying assumptions and values. Socialists sought a radical overhaul of existing property relations, involving the transfer of the private ownership of the means of production to social ownership, and a massive redistribution of income and wealth in favour of the working classes. This involved also a rejection of the free market values and competition lauded by liberals in favour of planning and co-operation. Most socialists instinctively felt that it should be possible to improve on the unplanned outcome of market forces under capitalism, with its periodic booms and slumps, involving unused capacity and human misery.

But although socialism in some ways was the very antithesis of liberalism, it also developed from liberalism. Both were products of the modern world – of the rise of science, industrialisation and associated political upheavals. In this manner, socialism shared with liberalism a post-Enlightenment rationalism, and optimism over progress. It adopted much of the liberal political programme, most notably for a reform and extension of the franchise, and the establishment of civil rights; and it embodied many liberal values, such as the familiar revolutionary triad, liberty, equality and fraternity, although giving them a markedly different interpretation.

Socialist values

Socialism is pre-eminently an ideology of equality, and it is the centrality of this value which marks it off from conservatism with its emphasis on hierarchy, leadership and natural inequality, and from liberalism, where a commitment to formal legal and political equality has not been extended to economic and social equality. Socialism involved from the beginning a fundamental critique of existing inequality under capitalism and a programme for a significant redistribution and equalisation of income, wealth and power.

Yet socialists have not always agreed over what this commitment to equality should involve in practice. For a few, it had involved the total abolition of personal private property, a solution anticipated by Plato for the Guardians of his ideal state, and by some religious communities. For many socialists it is, however, only the private ownership of the means of production which needs to be replaced by common ownership. The application of this principle has aroused acute debate. It has sometimes been interpreted by mainstream British socialists as public ownership of the 'commanding heights' of industry. There have also been considerable differences over exactly what common ownership entails in practice – for example, state ownership or workers' control.

Revisionist socialists, now often described as social democrats, have argued that the promotion of equality no longer requires wholesale nationalisation. According to this analysis, progressive taxation coupled with state welfare benefits will help to produce a more egalitarian society, although there is no very clear conception of how much inequality can be tolerated, or how far it is practical or desirable to push equality.

While both advocates and critics acknowledge that socialism is in some sense about equality, the importance attached to liberty is rather more contestable. As Tawney (1931, p. 164) suggests, 'Liberty and equality have usually in England been considered anti-thetic', and indeed conservatives and liberals have often accused socialists of sacrificing liberty to equality. Socialists have on the whole strenuously denied this, maintaining that equality is a condition of liberty. Equality does not mean uniformity, but rather frees individuals to develop their full and different potentials. The socialist commitment to liberty has been strongly re-emphasised by modern British Labour Party politicians (Hattersley, 1987). Socialists have also argued that the freedom celebrated by classical liberals is fairly meaningless in the context of severe economic and social deprivation and a culture which inevitably reflects the values of the dominant class. Like some New Liberals, socialists tend to see freedom in what has been termed a positive rather than a negative sense – freedom *to* enjoy something which is valued, rather than freedom *from* restraint and coercion. 'Liberty implies the ability to act, not merely to resist.' (Tawney, 1931, p. 165)

Critics have pointed to some inherent dangers in the notion of positive liberty, suggesting it may be used to justify coercion for people's own good (Berlin, 1958). Socialist planning clearly implies some curtailment of individual freedom, but of course, socialists would argue that freedom in a capitalist society is largely illusory for the majority, not only because choice is in practice severely constrained, but also because people do not necessarily recognise what is in their own best interest. Most socialists see human behaviour as essentially socially determined, the product of its environment, an assumption which cuts across a basic tenet of classical liberalism, that individuals know and pursue their own interests. For socialists, people's expressed interests are not necessarily their real interests, plausibly in view of assumptions concerning the social determination of attitudes and behaviour, and it follows that there may be some temptation for paternalist or bureaucratic interference with individual freedom, for the individual's own good as well as the perceived wider good of society.

The third term in the revolutionary triad – fraternity – has been less emphasised and analysed, but it is both important and problematic for socialism. Behind the notion of the 'brotherhood of man' lies an affirmation of the inherent worth of all humanity, regardless of class, nation, colour, creed, or (despite the somewhat sexist terminology) gender. But there is also an implicit assumption about the capacity of human beings to live peacefully and co-operatively with each other. This conception of man as essentially a social and, potentially at least, a selfless animal contrasts markedly with both conservative notions of a fatal flaw or evil streak in human nature and the competitive, self-seeking individualism which underpins liberalism. It is important, because it is upon this optimistic assumption concerning human nature that the feasibility of socialism essentially depends. It is also clearly problematic. Conservatives and liberals regard the socialist view of human nature as naive and unrealistic. Conservatives would claim it was invalidated by the abundant evidence of man's inhumanity to man over many centuries; liberals assume a need for rewards and incentives. Most socialists would reply that violent, competitive and acquisitive behaviour is socially determined – it is learned rather than natural. A socialist society would foster different values and behaviour.

Evolutionary and revolutionary socialism

If there are some differences among socialists over ultimate objectives, there are greater differences over how these objectives are to be achieved – not surprisingly, as socialism, unlike liberalism and conservatism, involved a radical alternative model of social and economic organisation for which there were initially no examples. Also, socialism implied a massive redistribution of income and wealth, and it was difficult to envisage the beneficiaries of the existing social and political system voluntarily relinquishing their property and power.

A fundamental distinction can be drawn between those favouring an evolutionary, gradualist route to socialism, relying on rational or moral persuasion, and those who, enthusiastically or reluctantly, endorse revolution. Evolutionary socialism has always been the

dominant strain in Britain, although ideas and analysis have sometimes been borrowed and adapted from the alternative revolutionary tradition.

Revolutionary socialism had been in part inspired by the example
of the French Revolution, which, although not essentially socialist,
had shown that an existing ruling class could be overthrown, and,
in so doing, had provided a precedent and inspiration for further
attempts to secure the transformation of society through insurrec-
tion. So there was, from the early nineteenth century onwards, a
strong tradition of revolutionary socialism, represented by such
figures as the French socialist, Blanqui (1805–81).

But many socialists rejected the revolutionary route to socialism.
It is worth emphasising that the legacy of the French Revolution was
somewhat ambivalent. It had disappointed many early enthusiasts
both in France and in other countries, for it had 'destroyed its own
children' and culminated in dictatorship. For many it was not an
example to be followed by a failure and a warning. This was perhaps
particularly so for British socialists. How far Jacobin sympathies in
Britain were eroded by the course of the revolution or by persecution is a moot point, but the fact that Britain was almost
continuously involved in war with revolutionary and Napoleonic
France from 1793 to 1815 must have strengthened a distrust for
revolution which was already arguably part of mainstream British
political culture, following the experience of the upheavals of the
seventeenth century.

Many early socialists hoped to build socialism peacefully, from
the bottom up, sometimes through ambitious attempts to establish
small-scale model socialist communities, but more usually through
practical experiments in mutual aid and self-help for working people,
such as the establishment of consumer and producer co-operatives,
friendly societies and trade unions, through participation in local
government, and through the encouragement of education. It could
be argued, however, that attempts to build socialism from the
bottom up, substantially ignored the problem of power. Such initia-
tives could not, in isolation, produce that fundamental transformation of society and the fundamental redistribution of income and
wealth which socialists sought. Marx and Engels attacked this form
of socialism as 'utopian', as there was no realistic strategy for its
achievement (*Communist Manifesto*, 1848).

Marx is clearly associated with the revolutionary route to

socialism, although it is worth emphasising that he was very critical of the revolutionary activities of such as Blanqui, viewing premature risings as pointless and counterproductive. Marxism is based on an analysis of underlying trends in the historical evolution of societies. Key elements in this historical evolution are classes, defined in terms of their relations with the means of production. In a capitalist society the crucial division was between the owners of capital, and the industrial proletariat who owned only their own labour. This fundamental conflict of interest could not be resolved and was bound to be intensified, as competition between capitalists would increase the exploitation and misery of the workforce. For Marx, a successful working-class revolution would be the inevitable consequence of the intensification of class conflict in a capitalist society.

Needless to say, it was Marx's revolutionary socialism which provided the inspiration for the Russian Revolution, and numerous other revolutions since that time, although neither the background circumstances, nor the actual course of these revolutions, have closely reflected Marx's own analysis. Lenin, in particular, provided his own gloss on Marx, extending the notion of a temporary dictatorship of the proletariat, and developing the concept of democratic centralism to establish an authoritarian, highly centralised state socialism.

In the meantime, an alternative evolutionary route to socialism, the parliamentary route, seemed increasingly plausible with the extension of the franchise to the working class in Britain and other liberal capitalist countries from the second half of the nineteenth century onwards. The parliamentary route involved the formation of new working-class socialist parties, competition for votes and parliamentary seats, and ultimately the capture of the apparatus of the state through a parliamentary majority. In this way, power could be won, and socialism established, through peaceful and democratic struggle. Indeed, for many, socialism seemed the natural corollary of democracy. Political equality would lead inexorably to social equality.

But although socialist parties were to enjoy considerable electoral success in Western Europe, progress towards socialism has been, for many socialist supporters, disappointing. Sometimes this has been ascribed to betrayal by the parliamentary leadership – a familiar complaint on the left. Indeed, it can be argued that there are endemic pressures to accommodation and compromise within the parliamentry system (Michels, 1949).

It could equally be argued that compromises with socialist objectives were necessary to win working-class votes. It was too readily assumed, both by early socialists and some of their opponents, that political democracy would lead rapidly to a major redistribution of income and wealth in favour of the masses. The extent to which the values of liberal capitalism were embedded in society as a whole was not appreciated, and the task of converting the working class to fundamentally different values in a hostile climate, was correspondingly underestimated (Coates, 1980).

Some would further argue that the parliamentary route to socialism inevitably involves a 'top-down', elitist, or paternalist approach, and results in a centralised state socialism which is the antithesis of the participative, co-operative values which were the essence of early socialist ideals. Attitudes to the state have varied markedly among socialists. At one end of the spectrum are anarchists who would totally reject the authority of the centalised state; at the other end are those who would, like Sidney Webb (1859–1947), identify the growth of state authority with socialism. Many socialists have argued, with Marx, that the existing state apparatus in a capitalist society inevitably reflects a narrow class interest and involves coercion, and must therefore be replaced by new institutions. But while Marx suggested that the state would 'wither away' after the revolution, Lenin and his successors developed a strong centralised state which showed few signs of withering. Western parliamentary socialists, while abhorring the Leninist state, have still tended to see socialism in terms of centralised state economic planning and collectivist state welfare provision. More decentralised, participative forms of socialism have been less evident.

Associated with this debate over the state there has also been within Britain as elsewhere a debate over the relative merits of parliamentary and extra-parliamentary (particularly industrial) action as a means to achieve social and political change. The trade unionism which was established in Britain from the second half of the nineteenth century onwards was predominantly legalistic, respectable, and limited to immediate practical objectives concerned with pay and conditions. It was, nevertheless, always possible to conceive of the use of industrial muscle to achieve wider economic and political ends. Syndicalists rejected parliamentarism in favour of such industrial action. Workers could thus use their power to seize control of industry. In theory this could be wholly non-violent. Disciplined strikes by workers in key industries, or a general strike, would immobilise the country and lead to a peaceful revolution. In practice it was likely that such industrial action would lead to violence. Furthermore, syndicalists have had a clear class conflict view of politics, so that syndicalism belongs more properly in the revolutionary rather than the evolutionary strand of socialism. Such revolutionary syndicalism has never been very strong in Britain, although it was influential before and after the First World War, up to the General Strike, which effectively destroyed its credibility. But watered-down syndicalism, in the form of Guild Socialism for example, has been a fairly consistent if subordinate strand in Labour Party thinking.

It should already be clear that radically different strategies for achieving socialism mask underlying differences over the analysis of existing society. Marxism involves a materialist interpretation of history, which suggests that political power and political development reflect economic and technological factors. Marxist economics involves in turn the assumption that inter-class relations are inevitably exploitative, that there is a fundamental and irreconcilable conflict of interest between capital and labour in a capitalist society. Other socialists, including most British socialists, have eschewed the language of class conflict. Free enterprise or *laissez-faire* capitalism is condemned as immoral and inefficient, with the implicit assumption that socialism is ultimately in the general or national interest rather than a class interest. It follows that even dominant interests in existing society may be persuaded of the benefits of socialism, a notion which, to the Marxist, is simply naive.

Working-class politics and early socialism in nineteenth-century Britain

As the first industrialising nation, Britain was the first country in which something like a modern industrial working class emerged. Previously, there were labouring classes, but not a working class conscious of its identity and collective interest. The labouring poor were indeed of only peripheral political significance. The London mob could be threatening, but was as likely to be roused in the cause of 'no popery' as for more radical objects. Industrialisation involved a new concentration of workers, both in workplaces and in new and fast growing urban settlements. This facilitated the communication of ideas, and organisation, and made the working class a factor in politics which could no longer be ignored.

There was certainly plenty of evidence of discontent among the labouring classes in Britain in the early stages of the Industrial Revolution. There was some revolutionary Jacobinism among tradesmen and artisans in the late eighteenth and early nineteenth centuries. There were the Luddite riots of 1811–13, involving machine breaking – an understandable reaction against the immediate impact of industrialisation on employment and working-class living standards. There were mass meetings and demonstrations, such as that broken up at Spa Field in Manchester in 1819 by cavalry. There were revolutionary plots, culminating in the 1822 Cato Street conspiracy. E. P. Thompson (1980) has woven all these and other strands together to produce a convincing picture of an emerging radical working-class consciousness, a picture perhaps reinforced by the trade union activity of the 1830s and still more by Chartism, a broadly-based working-class movement with radical political objectives, but involving a variety of ideas and strategies. Whether this expanding working class, increasingly conscious of its common interest, posed a real danger to the existing social order is debatable, although certainly some of the political establishment feared an intensifying class conflict and revolution.

Working-class radicalism did not necessarily involve socialism, but socialist ideas were advanced in the first half of the nineteenth century. Some had derived socialist conclusions from Ricardo's labour theory of value. The most influential British socialist in the first half of the nineteenth century was, however, Robert Owen (1771–1858).

Owen had demonstrated at New Lanark that it was possible to make money by enlightened capitalism, and at his more ambitious American model communtiy, New Harmony, that it was equally possible to lose a fortune. But even in his early years he was more than just an enlightened philanthropist. His work at New Lanark reflected a conviction which is characteristic of socialism, that people are moulded, for good or ill, by their environment. Such a view contradicted the conventional religious notion of personal moral responsibility, and Owen's irreligion soon lost him the respectful reputation he had briefly enjoyed in parliamentary circles. But as his influence with the political establishment declined, his reputation among the radical working class rose, and Owen was strongly associated with an ambitious spread of trade unions in the 1830s and the establishment of the co-operative movement in the 1840s.

Owen's legacy was considerable and controversial. Marx and Engels attacked him in the *Communist Manifesto*, grouping him with Saint-Simon (1760–1825) and Fourier (1772–1837) as a utopian socialist. The charge reflects his involvement in the move to establish model socialist communities cut off from the rest of the world and also the lack of a clear strategy to achieve socialism. Owen eschewed revolution, while his support for trade unionism and the co-operative movement could be comfortably accommodated within Victorian working-class self-help. In some ways the label 'utopian' seems unfair for a man who immersed himself in working-class politics and causes, and Engels later delivered another more generous verdict: 'Every social movement, every real advance in England on behalf of the workers links itself to the name of Robert Owen' (Marx and Engels, 1880).

Owen died in 1858, and from the 1850s both socialism and working-class militancy, following the collapse of Chartism, made little headway. The bulk of the British working classes apparently became imbued with the gradualist reformist parliamentary culture. Political and social reforms in the nineteenth century seemingly confirmed the existing system's capacity for change. Religious and other cleavages which cut across class divisions helped blunt social conflict. The benefits of early industrialisation and, more arguably, imperialism, improved living standards among elements of the working class, particularly from the mid-nineteenth century onwards when skilled craftsmen organised themselves into effective unions, which secured real improvements in pay and conditions and widened differentials with other workers (Gray, 1981). All this reduced hostility to the economic system, to the extent that accommodation within capitalism, rather than its wholesale transformation, was increasingly sought by leaders of the organised labour movement, many of whom saw no reason to go beyond radical liberalism in their political demands (Pelling, 1965, p. 6).

In marked contrast, then, with developments in France and Germany, socialist ideas were only weakly articulated in Britain in the period after 1848, and there was virtually no organised socialist activity before the 1880s (Pelling, 1965, pp. 13–15), by which time socialist ideas and socialist parties were already established with a mass following in several other European countries. Even after distinct socialist organisations emerged in Britain from the 1880s onwards, and ultimately a separate Labour Party, the influence of radical liberal thinking remained strong. Bentham, Mill, Hobhouse, and later Keynes and Beveridge, all arguably had a bigger influence on the character and development of British socialist thought than many thinkers with more authentic socialist credentials. In the main, British socialism grew out of radical liberalism, and has long continued to bear the marks of its origins.

Marxism and the British labour movement

The failure of British workers to develop a stronger class consciousness and a revolutionary social and political programme was noted sadly by two celebrated foreign observers of the British social and political scene in the second half of the nineteenth century. Marx and Engels (1820–95) spent the bulk of their working lives in England, studied conditions in England extensively and involved themselves in British working-class politics. Britain, as the most advanced capitalist country in their day, might have appeared the prime candidate for a Marxist-style socialist revolution. Despite all this, Marxist ideas have had less influence on the development of socialist thought in Britain than in Germany, France, Italy, Russia, China and many other countries where the ground for their reception might seem far less fertile.

Although the British authorities kept a watchful eye on the socialist agitator in their midst, they seem to have concluded that he was not particularly dangerous. Grant Duff, a Liberal MP who arranged a meeting with Marx at the suggestion of Queen Victoria's eldest daughter, enjoyed three hours civilised conversation with him and concluded, 'It will not be Marx who, whether he wishes it or not, will turn the world upside down' (McLennan, 1976, p. 445). While this was not among the more accurate historical prophecies ever made, it would have been less wide of the mark if applied exclusively to Britain.

The relatively weak influence of Marxist ideas in Britain can be largely attributed to factors already explored – political stability and a tradition of gradualism, a blurred and fluid class system, the existence in Owenism of a distinct native strand of socialism, the relative prosperity of sections of the working class, the extension of the franchise and the reforms apparently secured through parliamentarism, the acceptance of trade unionism by the political establishment, and the consequent movement of labour leaders towards accommodation within the existing economic and political system.

Several accounts have also stressed personal factors, particularly the eccentric and abrasive personality of Britain's leading native Marxist in the late nineteenth and early twentieth centuries. H. M. Hyndman (1842–1921) was a former Tory imperialist who managed to upset his mentors, Marx and Engels, and quarrel with most other leading socialists of his day (Pelling, 1965, pp. 18–32; Pierson, 1973, pp. 60–75; Callaghan, 1990, ch. 2). He was an able polemicist, but might have had more influence had he been less scathing about the theory and practice of trade unionism. His Social Democratic Federation (SDF) was the oldest, and in some ways the strongest, of the three socialist organisations which combined with trade unions to form the Labour Representation Committee in 1900, but left within a year and subsequently had only very marginal influence on the development of socialist ideas in Britain.

Of course, the spread of Marxist ideas in Britain was not just dependent on Hyndman. Marx's theories were familiar in British socialist circles, although not always fully understood or appreciated. William Morris (1834–96), while enjoying the historical parts of *Das Kapital* confessed that he 'suffered agonies of confusion of the brain over reading the pure economics of that great work' (Morris, ed. Briggs, 1962, p. 34). George Bernard Shaw (1856–1950) tried to convert his fellow Fabians to Marxist economics, but was soon persuaded to repudiate Marx in favour of the then orthodox economics of Jevons (1835–82) (Foote, 1986, p. 25). In general, early British socialism was eclectic, and Marx was only one influence among many.

Nor has that situation changed much subsequently. The Bolshevik revolution of 1917 naturally gave some impetus to renewed interest in Marxist ideas both inside and outside the Labour Party (Callaghan, 1990, ch. 7). However, the emergence of the Communist Party of Great Britain in 1920 from older small socialist groups, and the refusal of the Labour Party to allow the new body to affiliate to it, emphasised the split between revolutionary and evolutionary socialism, in Britain as elsewhere. The hardening division between western-style parliamentary socialism and soviet-style communism rendered Marxist analysis suspect in Labour circles. Moreover, the progress of the Labour Party in the 1920s, apparently confirmed the faith of the leadership in parliamentarism and constitutionalism.

Later, the economic collapse in 1931 led some British socialists like Strachey (1901–63) to question gradualism and embrace Marxism, and rendered the alternative soviet model of socialism more attractive, even to the high priests of British evolutionary socialism, Sidney and Beatrice Webb. Marxism and Russian-style communism were intellectually fashionable throughout the 1930s, but even so their influence on the leadership of the Labour Party and the bulk of the working class was fairly negligible (Pimlott, 1977). After 1945, the cold war and growing economic prosperity in the west again rendered Marxist analysis suspect or seemingly irrelevant. Strachey repudiated his earlier Marxist views (Foote, 1986, p. 210). Tony Crosland (1956, p. 2) was briefly dismissive: 'In my view Marx has little to offer the contemporary socialist either in respect of practical policy, or of the correct analysis of our society, or even of the right conceptual tools of framework.'

Since the revisionist heyday of the 1950s, Marxism has again become increasingly fashionable in left-wing academic circles, and has been articulated by a number of fringe left groups and parties. Sophisticated Marxist analysis has had some impact on thinking within the Labour Party, and at another level there have been highly publicised attempts at infiltration of constituency parties and trade unions by organisations such as the Militant Tendency and its more fundamentalist Marxism. Even so, it may still be argued that the real influence of Marxist ideas on the Labour Party both in the parliamentary party and the country has remained relatively weak (Coates, 1980, p. 163).

Trade unionism and labour representation

It is not the attractions of alternative forms of socialism which explains the weak influence of Marxism in Britain, but rather the strength and character of British trade unionism. This did not just limit the potential for the spread of Marxist ideas, but, some might argue, for any variant of socialism. Trade unions had been banned early in the nineteenth century, but had since been not only legalised, but to some extent also protected by the law. Early attempts by Robert Owen and others to establish a national general union of workers had ended in failure, and the first successful unions, set up from the mid-nineteenth century onwards, had been of skilled workers. These constituted something of a labour aristocracy (Gray, 1981) which had profited sufficiently from the existing economic system to resist the attractions of socialism. Socialist ideas were more prevalent among the leaders of groups of semi-skilled and unskilled workers, who became effectively organised for industrial purposes later in the century (Callaghan, 1990, ch. 4). Even so, the bulk of trade unionists seemed indifferent or hostile to socialism by the turn of the century and retained strong links with radical liberalism.

This is not so very surprising. British trade unionists were, of course, imbued with the reformist, parliamentary British political culture, which was reinforced by the apparent success of the working class in securing increased economic prosperity, and political and trade union rights. Trade unionism, moreover, implies some accommodation within capitalism rather than its transformation (Coates, 1980, p. 208). Indeed, trade union insistence on the right to free collective bargaining (effectively within a capitalist market order) involves potential for conflict with socialist planning. Even some welfare measures of the type advocated by gradualist socialists, such as family allowances, have from time to time aroused the hostility of the trade union movement because they reduce effective take-home pay and undermine the case for higher basic wages.

Trade unionism certainly did not imply socialism. Nor did it even involve necessarily separate labour parliamentary representation. Until the late nineteenth and early twentieth centuries, most trade unionists were content with the two established political parties, which, from self-interest, were increasingly sensitive to labour pressure. Several factors caused a change in outlook, including the reluctance of the established parties to endorse working-class candidates, some bitter industrial disputes in the early 1890s, and, most significantly, growing anxieties about the legal position of trade unions, following a series of disquieting cases in the courts (Pelling,

1965, p. 200). These doubts were not sufficient to impel more than a minority of unions to support separate labour representation in 1900. It was the impact of a particular court case in 1901, concerning a strike aganst the Taff Vale Railway Company, which persuaded most unions of the need for parliamentary representation (Pelling, 1965, pp. 213ff.). Affiliations to the infant Labour Representation Committee (LRC) trebled. Since then, the commitment of the vast bulk of the trade union movement to what was soon renamed the Labour Party has never been in serious doubt.

Yet the commitment remained initially (and, arguably, always essentially) to labour representation rather than socialism. What the trade unions wanted was a party to advance and defend the interests of unions in particular, and the working class more generally. There were, of course, already some reciprocal ties between trade unionism and socialism. Some individual trade union leaders and activists were, or called themselves, socialists, and the unions who joined the LRC were plainly prepared to enter an alliance with established socialist organisations, even if they were not prepared to commit the new party to socialist goals. Socialists, on the other hand, had given considerable encouragement and support to the New Unionism from the 1880s. But there were, all the same, considerable mutual suspicions. Hyndman's general hostility to what he saw as the limitations of trade union action led him soon to withdraw his SDF from the LRC, while the Fabians were patronising and disparaging about both the unions and the working classes (Adelman, 1986, p. 10).

It is scarcely surprising that some trade unionists were in turn critical of middle-class intellectual socialists whose commitment to trade unionism and the labour movement seemed, at best, doubtful. Despite the establishment of the separate party, many of the trade unionist MPs remained essentially liberal in attachments and ideology. The Labour Party in parliament seemed to operate as little more than a pressure group within the Liberal coalition before the First World War (Adelman, 1986, pp. 38–45).

Even after the Labour Party was formally committed to socialist objectives in 1918, there have been considerable doubts expressed over the depth of that commitment, and some would argue that the ideology of the Labour Party has remained essentially 'labourist' rather than socialist (Miliband, 1972, p. 61). The Labour Party, as Ernest Bevin graphically described it, emerged from the bowels of the trade union movement, and trade union interests remain strongly entrenched in the constitution of the party (Minkin, 1978, ch. 1). Because of its still huge affiliated membership, trade union delegates control the bulk of the votes at the Labour Party conference, directly or indirectly determine who should occupy the majority of places on the National Executive Committee, and following the Wembley conference of 1981, control 40 per cent of the votes for the election of the Labour leader and deputy leader. Beyond that, the trade unions remain effectively the paymasters of the Labour Party.

One, perhaps surprising, consequence of the continuing major role of trade unions in the British Labour Party has been to establish the primacy of parliamentary rather than industrial action as the strategy for the achievement of socialism. Once the Trades Union Congress (TUC) decided to back parliamentary representation, it committed the trade union movement wholeheartedly to parliamentarism. There were, of course, trade union leaders who were attracted to anarcho-syndicalist ideas and industrial action to achieve political objectives both before and after the First World War, but these were a minority within the trade union and labour movement. This was never more clearly demonstrated than in the 1926 General Strike, when the General Council of the TUC insisted that the strike was an industrial dispute rather than a strike against the government, and strove for a face-saving formula as an escape from a situation which they had not sought. The failure of the strike seemed to confirm to both the Labour parliamentary and trade unionist leadership the futility of industrial action for political purposes, and reinforced parliamentarism (Miliband, 1972, p. 151). Indeed, the trade unions became more committed than ever to the Labour Party, and until the mid-1950s provided consistent loyal support to the party's parliamentary leadership (McKenzie, 1963). So, the two wings of the labour movement were complementary rather than competitive, each content to leave the other supreme in its own sphere. It was only when this collaborative relationship began to break down from the late 1950s onwards that the latent tension between parliamentary and industrial action again resurfaced.

Labourism

The term 'labourism' implies an ideology which articulates the felt interests of labour, or the working class. To a very considerable extent the Labour Party was successful in establishing itself as a class party, seducing the bulk of the working class from their early allegiance to the established Liberal and Conservative Parties, although of course a significant minority has continued to vote Tory. But while Labour convinced most manual workers that the party was their party, looking after their interests, it may be doubted whether it ever converted most of them to socialism. It might well be argued that 'labourism' represents what Parkin (1972, p. 81) has described as a 'subordinate value system' promoting accommodation with the established social and political order, as opposed to a 'radical value system' providing a direct challenge to that order. In summary, workers wanted a party which would protect their trade union bargaining rights, raise their standard of living and provide certain benefits such as cheap public housing and free health care, but not necessarily a party which would challenge the whole basis of the economic and social system.

On the other hand, if socialism has never been wholeheartedly embraced by the British working class, even old-fashioned labourism has, arguably, become an ideology which has recently commanded less support, for a number of reasons. In the first place, both the parliamentary leadership of the Labour Party and even many constituency activists are no longer of the working class (Hindess, 1971). Secondly, and partly perhaps reflecting these social changes within the party, the policies pursued by Labour have not always appeared to benefit the working class. For example, the expansion of higher education in particular can be interpreted as an enormous boon to the middle class paid for out of the taxes of the community as a whole, including increasingly the working class. Finally, in recent years Labour has been represented as more interested in promoting equal opportunities for women, blacks or gays, than defending the interests of their traditional working-class clientele. Such perceptions may be exaggerated, but underline the extent to which the Labour Party is no longer automatically seen by many white, and predominantly male, manual workers as 'their' party.

More important than either of these developments within the

Labour Party are changes in the class structure and in class identification. The manual working class is itself relatively smaller, and more divided – for example, between public and private sector employees, between council tenants and owner-occupiers, and on gender and ethnic grounds. As the working class appears less homogeneous it is not surprising that there is less of a common working-class culture. The influence of greater affluence on attitudes has been a subject of academic interest since the 1950s. Now manual workers not only own cars and their own homes, and take holidays abroad, they may also have private health care and own shares. Such developments have arguably weakened what Parkin (1972, p. 91) described as the 'instrumental collectivism' of the bulk of the working class.

So the future of 'labourism' is problematic. The Labour Party once appeared more labourist than socialist. Now, while its socialism remains, as ever, a contestable issue, it no longer seems even labourist. This may be partly attributed to a middle-class takeover, but it also reflects the need of the party to widen its social base to survive. Labour began as an explicitly class party, with a programme pitched deliberately at the working class, although of course it always enjoyed some middle-class support and active involvement. The reduction in size and the fragmentation of the old manual working class means that Labour has to broaden its appeal. This suggests the need for some ideological revision, away from labourism. The implications for socialism are unclear.

The Labour Party and socialism

The Labour Party has always contained socialists, and since 1918 at least has been committed to socialist objectives. Yet the extent and nature of the Labour Party's socialism has been contentious since its origins. In marked contrast with some continental socialist parties which began as revolutionary socialist and became reformist over time, Labour began as a trade unionist reformist party which moved in the direction of socialism. Perhaps the Labour Party might never have advanced beyond the labourist or radical liberal ideology associated with its trade union origins – indeed, some critics would suggest that it never has done. But it was unlikely that trade unionism alone could provide a coherent philosophy for an enduring national political party, and the logic of radical liberalism was to undermine the need for a separate labour political organisation. Thus it was probable, if not inevitable, that the Labour Party would be driven eventually to an explicit commitment to the socialist goals that some of its members had always supported. For reasons already discussed it was most unlikely that the brand of socialism embraced would owe anything of significance to Marx. In fact, the socialism of the Labour Party was to be a blend of the ethical socialism particularly associated with the Independent Labour Party (ILP) and the gradualist and social scientific outlook of the Fabians.

Mainstream British socialism has rarely been associated with anti-clericalism. In fact, there has been a significant strand of Christian socialism within the British Labour movement. While the influence of the early Christian socialists such as Kingsley (1819–75) and Maurice (1805–72) was relatively slight and short-lived, there have been a succession of influential British thinkers who derived their socialism from their Christian convictions, including Tawney (1880–1962) and Cripps (1889–1952). At the same time, the strength of the Nonconformist tradition, and especially Methodism, in the labour movement has been widely acknowledged.

For many, socialism was not derived from religion, but almost a religion itself, and religious language and imagery was a pervasive element of much turn-of-the-century socialist propaganda. This was particularly true of the Independent Labour Party, founded by Keir Hardie in 1893, and one of the three socialist organisations which in 1900 joined with the trade unions to form the Labour Representation Committee. Hardie (1856–1915) who became the new party's first leader contrasted the 'glorious Gospel of Socialism' with the 'gospel of selfishness'. Religious imagery was common among socialists of the period (Greenleaf, 1983, Vol. II, p. 414; Callaghan, 1990, p. 67). The Glasiers published a book entitled the *Religion of Socialism* in 1890, and John Glasier subsequently referred to the 'sacrament of socialism' (quoted in Foote, 1986, p. 34). Such language came easily to working people brought up in an atmosphere of Christian evangelism in Nonconformist chapels, and served the same function of conversion to the faith, whether Christian or socialist. Philip Snowden, later Labour's 'Iron Chancellor', described the revivalist atmosphere of the ILP meetings of his youth in his autobiography. Working men 'went out into the streets to preach in their simple way the new gospel of emancipation.' There were choirs, and processions, and even proselytising cycling excursions into the countryside (quoted in Adelman, 1986, p. 107).

The religious atmosphere of meetings of the ILP and some other socialist groups may not have persisted, but a moralistic strain has been a feature of British labourist and socialist ideology down to the present day. Arguably, it has brought a fervour and commitment to the socialist case which has been a potent factor in winning and retaining mass support. The ethical socialists were also consciously articulating a new morality involving unselfish, co-operative behaviour, which made certain assumptions about human nature and potential, and involved a direct challenge to the self-interested individualist assumptions behind classical economics and *laissez-faire* liberalism. One aspect of the ethical approach was a universalism which emphasised the brotherhood of man, and rejected conflict and division. Thus Hardie explicitly rejected the Marxist doctrine of the class war, in which he has been followed by the mainstream British socialist tradition.

That tradition is also exemplified by R. H. Tawney who combined Christian convictions with historical scholarship and social analysis. His books, *The Acquisitive Society* (1921) and *Equality* (1931), influenced generations of British socialists. Although his writing is far more intellectually impressive than that of early ILP socialists, like them he eschewed the language of class war, revolution, and Marxism, and pinned his hopes especially on education to develop a new social consciousness.

The main weakness of ethical socialism was a certain intellectual fuzziness at its core. A thorough-going Marxist analysis was implicitly rejected, but there was little in the way of a convincing alternative theoretical foundation for socialism. Ethical socialism was long on commitment and evangelical fervour, but short on economic and social analysis. Foote's (1986, p. 37) verdict is brutal: 'It was basically a withdrawal from the world, and as such, it was impossible to translate into the practical politics of government.' There is something in this. Their socialist vision could win converts, and so help win power, but offered little guidance in using power. Millennial visions of the future were not much help in coping with the pressing problems of the present. This deficiency was in part supplied by another very different strand in British socialism, the Fabians.

In many respects the Fabians were the antithesis of the ILP. If the imagery and rhetoric of the ILP was moralistic and quasi-religious, the Fabians prided themselves on their rational and scientific approach to economic and social issues (Greenleaf, 1983, Vol. II, p. 392). While the ILP recruited working-class activists and aspired to become a mass party, the Fabians began as a small group of middle-class intellectuals, with ambivalent attitudes to working-class politics. The Fabian Society had been founded in 1884. It was named after the Roman General, Fabius Maximus Cunctator, who defeated Hannibal by patient delaying tactics (effectively refusing to fight him), and it adopted the emblem of the tortoise on its early publications. Both name and emblem were symbolic of a commitment to gradualist, non-revolutionary socialism. Beyond that, there was no party line, and the early Fabians contained a diversity of ideas and a rare array of intellectual talent, including two authors who were to establish a world reputation, Shaw and Wells, a celebrated children's writer, Edith Nesbit, an important if neglected social scientist, Graham Wallas, the neo-Malthusian, Annie Besant and the psychologist, Havelock Ellis. It was, however, Beatrice and Sidney Webb, who were to become most closely identified with Fabian socialism (Greenleaf, 1983, Vol. II, p. 381).

Some would deny that Fabian socialism involved socialism at all. If the objective of the common ownership of the means of production is regarded as the litmus test for socialists, then Sidney Webb (1859–1947), who drafted clause four of the Labour party's constitution in 1918, was a socialist. Those who would deny the label 'socialist' to the Fabians have focused on their gradualist parliamentarian strategy for achieving socialism rather than their objectives. The Webbs believed, like Marx, in the inevitable triumph of socialism, but whereas Marx saw this as the result of class conflict and revolution, the Webbs viewed it as the irresistible end product of the steady growth of state intervention in society, the 'inevitability of gradualness'. Lovingly, Sidney Webb (1889) chronicled all the activities once 'abandoned to private enterprise', now controlled or regulated by the state. While many continental socialists saw the existing state apparatus as the enemy, Webb tended to assume that the advance of the state was synonymous with the advance of socialism. Critics have suggested that Webb was far too ready to claim for socialism every trivial extension of state intervention, and to assume that socialism and collectivism were one and the same.

The Webbs believed the trend towards collectivism was irrevers-
ible, because state provision was manifestly more efficient than
private provision. Good government was essentially a matter of
applying the appropriate expertise, based on scientific research and
professional training (Greenleaf, 1983, Vol. II, pp. 397ff.). The
Webbs themselves were indefatigable researchers. They saw their
socialism as essentially dispassionate, rational and scientific.

By the same token it was also paternalist and elitist. The Fabians
have often been criticised for being middle class – rather unfairly,
as so were many other non-Fabian socialists. More to the point,
despite their early involvement in the Labour Party, there was
initially little faith in trade unions or the working class. Socialism
was to be applied from the top down for the benefit of the working
class, rather than won by pressure from below. Their vision of
socialism involved scientific administration by disinterested, properly trained and qualified civil servants, and owed more to the
British utilitarian tradition than to continental socialism. It was to
be achieved by rational persuasion – the Webbs hoped their ideas
would permeate society, including particularly the current political
establishment, and they pressed their recommendations on leading
Liberal and Conservative politicians, at least in the period before
1914.

This rational, scientific and paternalist socialism was very different from the evangelical and populist socialism of the ILP. However, despite these differences, the ideas of the ethical and Fabian
socialists were not incompatible. Both had their roots in strands of
liberalism – the Fabians in utilitarianism, the ILP in Nonconformist
radicalism. Both wished to transcend the radical liberal tradition
and the labourism associated with trade unionism. Yet both at the
same time rejected the class war, and Marxism. Both were parlia-
mentarist, and, despite the millennial rhetoric employed by the
ethical socialists, essentially gradualist. Their role within the Labour
Party was, until 1918 at least, complementary rather than competitive. The ILP was the recruiting agent, trying to win the working
class for socialism, the Fabians were more an intellectual think-
tank, carrying out policy-oriented research.

After 1918, and the establishment of a national organisation for
the Labour Party, with individual membership, the ILP lost its distinctive role in recruitment, and became effectively a party within
a party. The resulting tension between a reformist parliamentary

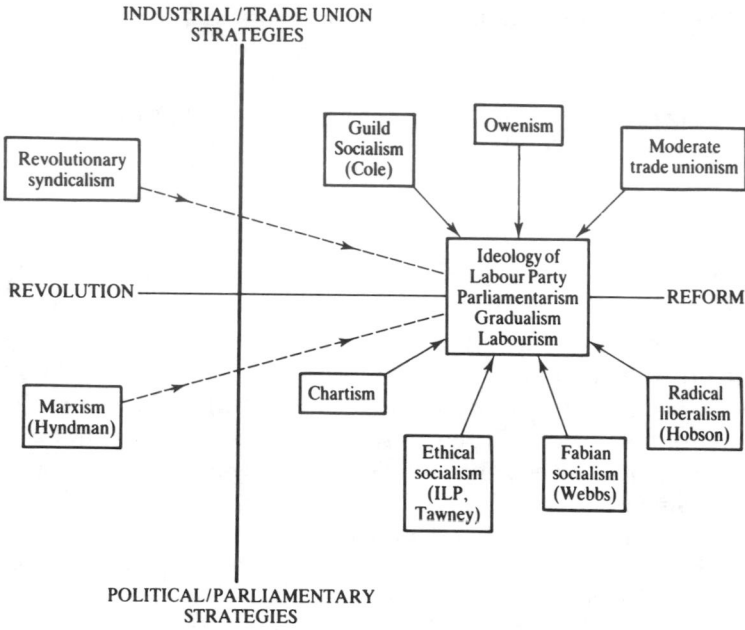

INDUSTRIAL/TRADE UNION
STRATEGIES

Revolutionary
syndicalism

Guild
Socialism
(Cole)

Owenism

Moderate
trade unionism

REVOLUTION

Ideology of
Labour Party
Parliamentarism
Gradualism
Labourism

REFORM

Marxism
(Hyndman)

Chartism

Radical
liberalism
(Hobson)

Ethical
socialism
(ILP,
Tawney)

Fabian
socialism
(Webbs)

POLITICAL/PARLIAMENTARY
STRATEGIES

Note: The strands of thought influencing the ideology of the Labour Party are here represented along two dimensions. The horizontal axis indicates roughly where movements or thinkers might be located on a revolution/reform spectrum. The vertical axis represents the distinction between industrial/trade union strategies and political/parliamentary strategies. However, it should be appreciated that particular tendencies and even individual thinkers involve a range of ideas, and often considerable ambiguities, so that too much should not be read into specific locations on the diagram.

Figure 5.1 Influences on the ideology of the Labour Party

leadership and an increasingly critical and radical-left ILP led ultimately to disaffiliation from the Labour Party in 1932. Its influence was subsequently marginal.

By contrast, the Fabian Society, eclectic and undoctrinaire, has continued to provide a forum for ideas and a research capacity for the Labour Party until the present day. This has been its strength. Its weakness might be that very eclecticism which has made it receptive to new ideas and research agendas. For example, it has never developed a coherent economic and social theory to provide an intellectual alternative to Marxism. Nor has it even evolved much in the way of lower-order partial theories which might be of practical benefit to Labour governments. Therefore, while the

Fabians cannot be accused of neglecting economics they have not produced a distinctive brand of Fabian economics, but rather have drawn extensively from fashionable and largely non-socialist economists, unsurprisingly leading to prescriptions which have tended to reflect the professional consensus of the day. Ultimately, the Fabians have been no more successful than the ILP in supplying an intellectually coherent alternative form of socialism to Marxism.

State socialism and alternatives to state socialism

Labour Party socialism has often been described as centralised state socialism. Fabianism undoubtedly contributed to this emphasis on the centre despite its association with 'gas and water socialism', the Webbs' own early involvement in the politics of the London County Council and their academic study of local government. It was thus not only parliamentarism, but centralised state socialism which was effectively endorsed in the 1920s, rather than alternative approaches such as Guild Socialism.

This trend was reinforced by the subsequent interpretation of the celebrated clause four, and its commitment to common ownership, drafted by Sidney Webb. Although this became a fixture in the Labour Party's political programme there was no clear conception of how it was to be undertaken and implemented. It was Herbert Morrison (1888–1965), both in the LCC in the 1930s, and subsequently in the post-war Labour government, who established the public corporation as the vehicle for Labour's programme of public ownership. Accordingly, all the industries nationalised by Labour from 1945–51 were established as public corporations, as was steel when it was renationalised in 1967, and the Post Office when it was reorganised in 1968. Other methods of nationalisation used abroad were not explored. There was nothing particularly new or socialist about the public corporation, a model which had been used for the British Broadcasting Corporation in 1926. Although the public corporation was wholly state-owned, it did not involve workers' control, or consumer participation, but, essentially, management on ordinary commercial lines, in some cases by chairmen recruited from successful private sector industry. Some socialist critics, perhaps unsurprisingly, dismissed Labour's public sector as 'state capitalism'.

Centralising tendencies within the Labour Party were reinforced by two world wars, particularly the second, when Labour was closely involved in both wartime planning and post-war reconstruction. Perhaps it was inevitable in the interests of equity that the post-war system of social security should be organised on bureaucratic lines under a strong central department, although it should be noted that there had been previously a strong local input into the administration of poor relief. What was less inevitable was that the new National Health Service involved the removal of hospitals from local government control, and paved the way for an administration of the service which was progressively removed from any significant local democratic control or influence. This proved significant. For a variety of reasons Labour in power has contributed to the erosion of local autonomy which has been a marked feature of the post-war years (Blunkett and Jackson, 1987, p. 64).

Acceptance of Keynesian economic theory arguably reinforced the trend to centralism. This may seem an odd claim, as the adoption of Keynesian planning was at the expense of more socialist, and perhaps more centralist, forms of economic planning. Keynes himself, although a critic of previous orthodoxy, had never been a socialist. His approach to economic planning, far from involving the abandonment of capitalism, was designed to remove its more obvious defects and effectively preserve it. Yet Keynesian-style planning assumed overall central guidance by disinterested Treasury mandarins, which was thoroughly consistent with Sidney Webb's brand of paternalist socialism. Keynesian economics also involved active state intervention at the level of the national economy. Full employment, for example, could be maintained by controlling aggregate demand, without requiring specific state intervention at the micro-level of particular industries, firms or localities.

Even when Keynesian economic remedies appeared to be less effective in the 1960s and 1970s, Labour governments if anything became more centralist, seeking the active co-operation of both the TUC and Confederation of British Industries (CBI) in economic, industrial and welfare policies. This 'tripartism' or 'corporatism' involved a top-down policy-making process, which reduced the scope for the participation of backbench Labour MPs, ordinary party members, shop-floor workers, and local councils.

How far there was ever a realistic alternative to the centralised state socialist model is debatable. As has been noted, the roots of early British socialism lay in grass-roots working-class self-help.

The socialism of Robert Owen and, later, William Morris, was bound up with the life and work of ordinary people, not with national economic plans. The co-operative movement, in which Owen had played a leading part, was an effective practical demonstration of what could be achieved by mutual action, although in Britain the movement was effectively confined to the development of consumer co-operatives. Producer co-operatives, which have thrived in some other countries, have never been a significant feature of the British industrial scene, and have only recently rearoused the interest of British socialists. Socialists were also actively involved in local government from the late nineteenth century onwards, and some Labour councils tried to pursue radical socialist municipal policies, notably at Poplar in the 1920s, where generous wage rates and welfare provision were declared illegal by the courts.

An early significant challenge to centralised state socialism came from Guild Socialism, a peculiarly British mixture of medieval romanticism, watered-down syndicalism, and participative democracy (Greenleaf, Vol. II, 1983, pp. 417ff.; Foote, 1986, ch. 6). An early element, derived from Ruskin, Morris and the arts and crafts movement, was revulsion against industrialism, and a demand for the revival of traditional craftsmanship, with skilled craftsmen organised in guilds, as in the Middle Ages. What was to become a more potent and significant influence were the syndicalist ideas which had helped stimulate a rash of strikes in the years immediately preceding the First World War. Syndicalism had been fed by disillusion with the record of the pre-war Labour parliamentary party, and distaste for the paternalist state socialism of the Fabians. It was G. D. H. Cole (1889–1959) who wove these rather unpromising elements together into an intellectually coherent theory. Guild Socialism as propounded by Cole involved a compromise with, rather than an alternative to, Fabian collectivism, for Cole, unlike the revolutionary syndicalists, rejected neither the state nor parliamentarism. Parliamentary democracy needed to be supplemented with industrial democracy, rather than replaced by it, and Cole opposed the syndicalist notion of a revolutionary general strike.

Guild Socialist ideas were perhaps most influential immediately after the First World War, but thereafter faded. More recently, some disillusion with centralised state socialism has led to a revival of interest in municipal or local socialism (Boddy and Fudge, 1984), in industrial democracy and in the theory and practice of co-operatives

(Greenleaf, 1983, Vol. II, p. 527). Arguably, none of these had received much encouragement from post-war Labour governments. Experience since 1979, however, perhaps only underlines the problem of building socialism from the bottom up in a hostile national environment.

Socialism and revisionism

Any analysis of both the essence and limits of the socialism of the Labour Party should involve an investigation of the record of the 1945–51 Labour government. In retrospect this was the most successful and the most socialist of Britain's Labour governments. It was also the first to possess a clear parliamentary majority and a clear mandate. In a few years it laid the foundations of the Welfare State and the mixed economy, which were to survive relatively unchanged for a generation. Yet it is also clear that Labour's programme was strictly limited, and virtually exhausted well before the party lost power in 1951.

Opposition provoked a long internal battle for the party's soul and future between the left under Aneurin Bevan (1897–1960) and an increasingly revisionist right-wing leadership, particularly over defence and the symbolic issue of clause four, and the commitment to the common ownership of the means of production. The most coherent and articulate case for a restatement of socialist philosophy and objectives came from Anthony Crosland (1918–77). In *The Future of Socialism* (1956) he argued that a capitalist economy had been effectively transformed into a mixed economy, and that ownership of the means of production was no longer critical, as the key decison-makers were salaried managers, and Keynesian theory provided the tools for the regulation of the economy in the public interest. The development of a variety of forms of ownership would be preferable to wholesale nationalisation. Nationalisation should only be regarded as a means to an end. The socialist objective should be the pursuit of equality, which could be more effectively achieved through progressive taxation and the distribution of social benefits financed from economic growth.

The death of the revisionist Gaitskell in 1963, and the succession to the leadership of the candidate of the Bevanite left, Harold Wilson, did not signal the adoption of a more full-blooded socialism. In

fact the 1964–70 and 1974–9 Labour governments involved little
more than an increasingly desperate defence of the legacy of the
Attlee government, although the interval of opposition from 1970
to 1974 saw some socialist rethinking (Holland, 1975), and a renewed commitment to common ownership and planning which
eventually proved to involve more rhetoric than substance.

Critics have raised the perennial cry of betrayal by the leadership,
while apologists have pointed to economic constraints, and the lack
of clear parliamentary majorities. But it could be argued that the
programme of British socialism had been largely fulfilled by the
Attlee government. That government's record was not the first
instalment of a planned socialist transformation of the British
economy and society, but the culmination of that mixture of radical
liberalism, trade unionism and Fabianism which was the essence
of British socialism. Crosland's 'revisionism' thus involved not a
repudiation of Labour's socialist past, but a rationalisation and
celebration of the Attlee record. Wilsonian pragmatism reflected
a general absence of new ideological objectives within the party,
which appeared increasingly defensive and conservative.

Democratic socialism and social democracy

The Labour Party has always contained a tension between left and
right, between socialism and reformism. At times that tension has
surfaced into open and bitter conflict, as in the 1930s and 1950s,
while at other times it has been masked or controlled. Only in the
1980s has it threatened to destroy the coalition which is the Labour
Party. A substantial breakaway from the parliamentary Labour
Party in 1981 established the Social Democratic Party.

The breach was prefaced and apparently provoked by a swing to
the left within Labour which became marked after the election
defeat of 1979. It seemed then as if the British political scene was
becoming sharply polarised, with a pronounced shift to the right
within the Conservative Party mirrored by a parallel ideological shift
towards left-wing socialism by Labour. Yet while the Thatcherite revolution was remarkably successful in transforming the programme and character of the Conservative Party, the socialist
transformation of Labour proved temporary and largely illusory.

The Labour left associated particularly with Tony Benn has some similarities with the Bevanite left of the 1950s, yet it was an essentially new phenomenon. Indeed, many surviving members of the old Bevanite or Tribunite left could neither understand nor support it. Several factors, some contradictory, contributed to the various strands of what was never a homogeneous movement.

One was the apparent failure of Keynesianism, which had been a critical element in the revisionist socialism of Crosland and others. It seemed that Keynesian demand management could not secure the high rates of economic growth which would facilitate the painless movement towards a more equal society and more welfare provision. Worse, it could no longer apparently keep either unemployment or inflation in check. Moreover, the domestic economy seemed increasingly vulnerable to international pressures, and not amenable to Keynesian style planning. Thus the intellectual core of revisionism was destroyed. In place of the old economic policy instruments, socialist economists devised an Alternative Economic Strategy.

Closely associated with this apparent failure of Keynesianism was disillusion with the record of recent Labour governments and the associated parliamentary leadership. This provoked a strong drive to secure democracy within the party through constitutional reforms. It also re-awakened a hostility to parliamentarism which has periodically featured on the socialist left, and a suspicion of the corporatist arrangements which the Wilson and Callaghan governments had entered into. One consequence was a renewed interest in establishing socialism from the bottom up – through co-operatives for example. A 'New Urban Left' attempted sweeping radical reforms in local government, prompting academic discussion of local socialism.

Suspicion of parliamentarism chimed in with a more militant trade unionism which had been partly stimulated by Wilson's flirtation with trade union reform and adoption of incomes policy. Strongly represented in the increased industrial militancy were public sector and white-collar unions which had not previously been so significant within the trade union movement. There was some associated revival of old syndicalist and Guild Socialist ideas.

If militant trade unionism in some senses represented the old Labour working class, the left coalition also included more recent political tendencies reflecting social and economic change, such as the woman's movement and a growing political articulation of the concerns of ethnic minorities. A revived peace movement which drew notably on feminist support was part of an increasing interest on the left in green issues.

Over and above all these developments, the Labour Party became more susceptible to the influence of Marxist ideas. At one level Marxist academics provided convincing explanations of the failures of Labourism, and an extensive analysis of both corporatism and Thatcherism. At another level there was a determined effort by a particularly doctrinaire vulgar Marxist faction, the Militant Tendency, to infiltrate the party. In between, a number of radical socialists, sympathetic to a broadly Marxist analysis, who had previously despaired of the Labour Party, considered that it might after all be a credible vehicle for socialism, and joined or rejoined its ranks.

A leadership focus for this coalition of a new left within the Labour Party was provided by Tony Benn. Like Keith Joseph in the Conservative Party, Benn had repudiated the whole approach of the Governments of which he had been a part. Benn himself derived his socialist inspiration from Christianity rather than Marxism, and belongs to the British ethical socialist tradition (Benn, 1980; Foote 1986). Like earlier leaders of the Labour left, his principal support came from constituency activists, and he was distrusted by the parliamentary Labour Party, perhaps unsurprisingly in view of his criticism of parliamentarism.

All these developments provoked some alarm on the parliamentary right of the party. A series of events demonstrated that the left was now in the ascendancy – a commitment to take Britain out of the EEC, the defeat of Callaghan's heir apparent, Dennis Healey, by the old Bevanite and unilateralist, Michael Foot, in the 1980 leadership election, and a special conference which endorsed sweeping constitutional reforms within the party, including the introduction of an electoral college for future leadership elections and mandatory reselection procedures for sitting MPs. This precipitated the final rupture. Four former Labour cabinet ministers, Roy Jenkins, Shirley Williams, Bill Rodgers and David Owen, set up a new party, the SDP, which was soon joined by another two dozen sitting Labour MPs.

The split naturally entailed some redefinition of ideological position both among those who broke away from the Labour Party and those who remained. 'Social democrat' had for some time been a convenient label for describing reformist or revisionist socialists, although ironically, it had once been the preferred name for revolutionary Marxists. 'Democratic socialism' became an umbrella term for the Labour left. Such semantic nuances came to loom large.

A common accusation against the SDP was that they were attempting to construct, not an essentially new party, but a Mark II Labour Party. Indeed, they claimed to be the true heirs of Attlee and Gaitskell, and adopted the name of the Labour thinker, Tawney, to describe their newly created rival to the Fabian Society. Their leaders alleged that they had not left the Labour Party, but that the Labour Party had left them, implying a marked ideological shift to the left by Labour. The SDP programme involved, critics alleged, a new yesterday – support for the EEC and NATO, modified Keynesianism, the Welfare State, and incomes policy. The only essentially new policy proposal was constitutional reform, particularly electoral reform, a commitment which owed much to their new allies, the Liberals. Although there was a considerable intellectual ferment, including a spate of new books by prominent social democrats defining and redefining their ideological position, the only potentially important 'new' idea was the social market, and this was essentially derived from the post-war 'German economic miracle' associated with Erhard.

The SDP failed to make good their claim to old mainstream Attlee-type socialism, as most Labour 'moderates' in Parliament, and the vast bulk of Labour councillors, active members, and trade unionists, declined to join them. The new members they attracted were largely 'political virgins' – not previously closely identified with any old political party, and enthusiastic about a wholly new party with a new style and approach. Yet the SDP leaders' preoccupation with past battles within the Labour Party bedevilled any project to establish a new party with a new philosophy and programme. As a result of their failure either to capture the 'moderate' Labour faction or to forge a new political ideology, the SDP was eventually obliged to choose between submerging their identity within the Liberals, or political extinction.

Meanwhile, the left's triumph within the Labour Party, which had provoked the SDP breakaway, proved short-lived (Seyd, 1987). The extent of the left takeover had perhaps always been exaggerated, for the reformist right, even weakened by defections, had remained strongly entrenched in the party, and was able to enlist the support of some of the old Tribunite left in defence of parliamentary socialism. The crushing defeat in the 1983 election, which had been fought on a 'thoroughly Bennite platform' (Callaghan, 1990, p. 227), led immediately to a change in leadership and more gradually to an extensive policy revision, which gathered pace after the 1987 defeat. Opposition to the EEC gave place to enthusiasm for it. Unilateral nuclear disarmament was dropped. Extensive commitments to extend public ownership were quietly abandoned, and it was not even clear how far Labour was committed to reversing the Thatcher government's privatisation programme. Some of the Conservative changes in trade union law were explicitly endorsed. There was even an acceptance of continuing high levels of unemployment. Within a few years, the radical socialism of the early 1980s had apparently given way to a more timid social reformism than had characterised the despised Wilson and Callaghan era.

This extensive ideological revision has taken place against a background of developments which seem to have fundamentally altered the British political terrain. Profound changes in the economy involving a rapid decline in employment in traditional manufacturing and mining have reduced the old working class in size and power. This, coupled with government legislation, has reduced trade union militancy, and led to a 'new realism' in industrial relations. The erosion of the autonomy of local government has undermined Labour's power base in the big cities, and the scope for 'local socialism'. The dependence of the working class on collective provision has been weakened by economic and social trends which have been actively assisted and promoted by the Thatcher government. All this has arguably contributed to a shift in British political culture, in which the values of the market, competition, and enterprise have become more widely endorsed, a trend reinforced by the repudiation of centralised state socialism and planning in Eastern Europe following the revolutions in 1989.

In this context fundamentalist socialism of the Bennite type does not seem a credible alternative. But at the same time a return to the 'moderate consensus politics' of the 1950s and 1960s is not an option either. Mrs Thatcher's brand of Conservative radicalism has broken that consensus, and forced some reassessment of Labour's philosophy and commitments. The party can no longer simply defend the Attlee inheritance. Whether it is capable of constructing a convincing new analysis and programme which can win popular support remains to be seen.

6

The Far Left and the Far Right

Extremism and the British political tradition

The mainstream British political tradition has already been characterised as one which eschewed extremism and revolution. There have, of course, been individual thinkers and politicians, movements and parties outside that mainstream tradition, but they have had to contend with the whole weight of a political culture which has emphasised moderation and parliamentarism, and have thus failed to make more than a marginal contribution to the British political scene.

A conventional left-right political spectrum places communists, Trotskyists, and perhaps anarchists on the extreme left, and fascists on the extreme right. These creeds, then, are at opposite ends of the political spectrum. The seating in a continental legislature would serve to emphasise the point, with communists and their allies on the far left, and fascists or neo-fascists on the far right.

Such an approach assumes that there is some considerable affinity on the one hand between the communists and other parties of the left, such as parliamentary socialists, and on the other hand between fascists and traditional nationalists or conservatives. Indeed, this has sometimes seemed obvious in practice on the European continent, with examples of 'popular fronts' containing communists, socialists and other left groups, and parliamentary alliances between fascists and Nazis with nationalists and conservatives, of the sort that brought both Mussolini and Hitler to power. In Britain, the

150

relative insignificance of communists and fascists, in parliamentary terms at least, has ruled out the need for any formal collaboration, and the relationship has involved rather allegations of penetration and hidden influence. In this fashion, the Communist Party and various Trotskyist groups have from time to time sought to join or infiltrate the Labour Party, which in turn has had to counter a series of 'red scares' launched by its opponents who have tried to associate Labour with Communism. Fascist attempts to infiltrate the Conservatives have apparently been less systematic and less successful, although a number of individual members of extreme right groups have later been active in the party. More to the point perhaps has been the apparent sympathy of some leading Conservatives with the views of fascist groups on race and immigration.

Yet there is a view that the far left and the far right have more affinity with each other than those who are apparently closer on the political spectrum. This is a view articulated in its most sophisticated form in the theory of totalitarianism, which was particularly fashionable in America at the height of the cold war. Fascism and communism were seen as opposite sides of the same coin. Both were ideologies which required the total subordination of the individual to the state, where no independent organisations such as churches, unions, or other political parties were allowed to operate freely. The theory of totalitarianism was developed by Popper (1962), Talmon (1960) and Arendt (1967). Although it was held to be a peculiarly twentieth-century phenomenon, influences were discerned in the ideas of Plato, Rousseau and Hegel among others. The fiction of Orwell, Huxley and Kafka provided convincing and awful warnings of the nature of totalitarian society.

The notion of totalitarianism is now not so intellectually fashionable. There is less confidence in the freedom and individuality fostered by western pluralist democracies, so that the simple contrast between pluralism and totalitarianism is seen in less stark and complacent terms. Ideology, once viewed as the particular preserve of totalitarian systems, is now seen as all-pervasive. There is also a greater appreciation of the differences between soviet-style Communism and fascism. The most obvious and most fundamental distinction is that the fascists, despite their radical rhetoric, did nothing to demolish the capitalist economic system. Altogether, the notion of totalitarianism is no longer found to be a useful tool of analysis, and in retrospect is widely viewed as the product of ideological thinking.

However, it is not necessary to swallow the theory of totalitarianism to detect some similarities between the far left and the far right, both in general and, more specifically, in the British context. Both are outsiders, against the political system, and against the prevailing political culture. Both have therefore been seen, not surprisingly, as subversive by mainstream parties which broadly share that prevailing political culture. Both have something of a persecution complex, and from time to time have suffered real persecution. Both have presented the other as the real enemy, but to a degree both need each other as bogeymen and targets. And in Britain, both have exaggerated the significance of the other: Communism was widely proclaimed in the 1930s as 'the only alternative to fascism', and the far right has frequently blamed 'Communist subversion' for Britain's real or imagined ills.

Another interesting similarity in the British context is that both the ideologies of the far left, particularly the orthodox Communist variant (Callaghan, 1987, p. 28), and British fascism (Payne, in Laqueur, 1979, p. 309), are substantially imported creeds, with little specifically British intellectual contribution. But that is hardly surprising as there was little intellectual sustenance for either creed to draw from the British political tradition. In turn, their 'alien' nature has severely reduced their prospects of making serious headway in British politics. In France, for example, both far right and far left could tap into a deep well of popular consciousness – the right into monarchism, Bonapartism, Catholicism, and the values and traditions of the army; the left into the revolutions of 1789 and 1848, the Paris Commune of 1870–1, and the values and symbols of republicanism. France was a deeply divided society which was more receptive to sharply polarised political ideologies – to both communism and a variety of fascist or quasi-fascist movements. In Britain, it is possible to dispute the nature and extent of political consensus, but the broad apparent agreement on the core institutions and values associated with the political system would seem to make things very difficult for parties and movements outside that political consensus.

The far left

The 'far left' is a convenient umbrella term for describing a number of communist, left-wing socialist, and anarchist groups, and it is thus difficult to generalise about a 'far left' political ideology. But most, if not all, of the far left would share a commitment to revolutionary rather than evolutionary socialism, and it is this which distinguishes the far left in Britain, conceptually at least, from mainstream British socialism and labourism.

In many other western countries, such as France, Italy, Spain, and Germany, mass communist, revolutionary socialist, or anarchist parties, have been established. In Britain no such party or movement has come near to achieving comparable success. The Communist Party of Great Britain reached its high watermark in 1945, with the election of two MPs, who both lost their seats in 1950. No other separate left-wing party has even approached that very limited achievement.

The extent to which the relative weakness of the far left in Britain can be simply ascribed to unhelpful circumstances and the prevailing liberal democratic consensus is a question which has already been touched upon. At the same time, the far left has arguably contributed to its own impotence. In the first place, the far left in Britain has long been riddled with internal dissension. Relative insignificance has never seemingly inhibited the far left from indulging in frequent splits, purges, fierce doctrinal disputes, and vituperative personality conflicts, which have sapped energies and diverted attention away from more positive work. Secondly, an obsession with Leninist doctrinal orthodoxy, shown not only by the Communist Party, but by its various Trotskyist and Maoist rivals, has inhibited the development of a Marxist-based analysis more relevant to British politics and society (Callaghan, 1987). The same doctrinal orthodoxy has also made it more difficult for established left groups to respond to new political currents in British society, such as feminism, environmentalism, and black consciousness. Thirdly, despite the involvement of a number of colourful personalities in far-left groupings, no outstanding British socialist thinker or political leader has emerged on the non-Labour left to provide the focus for a mass movement. Significantly, the far left has always had to rely on left-wing Labour politicians, such as Cripps, Bevan, and Benn, to provide leadership and inspiration for broad left crusades.

The strategy of far-left groups has been born out of impotence, and has involved repeated oscillations between seeking formal affiliation within the Labour Party, through various forms of informal infiltration or 'entryism', to establishing a totally separate and rival party organisation in competition with Labour. The Communists have campaigned intermittently for formal affiliation with Labour, and have at times deliberately pursued entryist tactics, while at other periods have eschewed any connection with Labour's 'social fascists' or 'bourgeois reformists'. Trotskyist groups have sometimes worked openly within the Labour Party (International Marxist Group, and until 1965, International Socialists). Sometimes they have sought to infiltrate secretly into the Labour Party (Socialist Labour League, Revolutionary Socialist League and the Militant Tendency). Sometimes they have formally withdrawn from the Labour Party to establish their independence, and perhaps a separate political party (Workers' Revolutionary Party, Socialist Workers' Party). None of these strategies has been attended with any marked success, although Militant infiltration of some constituency Labour parties became the subject of some concern within the Labour Party and considerable media hype outside it in the mid-1980s.

Communism

The Communist Party was founded in 1920, and involved a fusion of earlier Marxist groups, such as the British Socialist Party (formerly Hyndman's Social Democratic Federation) and the Socialist Labour Party. There was thus an indigenous strand of Marxism which might have been drawn upon, but in practice the Russian Revolution, and Lenin's interpretation of Marx and Engels, became the paramount influences on the British party (Challinor, 1977). It was Lenin's ideas which became the new orthodoxy – the leading role of the party, 'democratic centralism', soviets, or workers' councils, rather than bourgeois parliamentarism, imperialism as the higher stage of capitalism. All other approaches to socialism were condemned, their exponents regarded as apologists for capitalism or 'social fascists'. The Soviet Communist leadership required total allegiance to the principles of Leninism. Not only were earlier British Marxists virtually forgotten, but other western Marxists were ignored, and the writings of Marx and Engels only known and understood through the prism of orthodox Leninism. It was assumed that the apparently successful Russian experience could be transplanted to British soil, and little attempt was made to interpret and apply Marxist theory to British or, indeed, Western European circumstances. From the foundation of the party through to the 1960s it was assumed that the Soviet leadership was almost beyond criticism, and the British Communist leadership loyally followed the Moscow line through every sharp policy reversal on doctrine, relations with other parties such as Labour, and foreign affairs.

The almost slavish loyalty to Moscow through the period of the purges and the show trials, the Nazi–Soviet pact, the post-war Russian domination of Eastern Europe, coincided with the relatively most successful period of British Communism. The slump seemed to confirm prophecies of the imminent collapse of capitalism. Visitors to the Soviet Union reported enthusiastically on the new civilisation in the making, while reports of purges were dismissed as exaggerated or anti-soviet propaganda. The threat of fascism, and active Communist involvement to counter that threat, notably in Spain, and from Mosley's supporters in the East End of London, led some to conclude that only the Communists could be relied upon to oppose the fascist menace. While the Nazi–Soviet pact inevitably led to some disillusionment on this score and a marked exodus from the party, this was soon forgotten when Stalin's Russia was invaded by Germany, and became instantly a valued ally.

Communism was intellectually fashionable through the 1930s until the end of the war. It was in this period that membership expanded to a peak of around 64,000 in 1942 (Callaghan, 1987, p. 48). Yet the influence of the party was never confined to its formal membership. At one level, this was the time when a number of young establishment intellectuals were recruited to work as undercover agents for the party, a role which some continued to perform with a remarkable dedication for the rest of their lives. At another level, it was in this period also that the party became influential in a number of trade unions, and won some wider sympathy and support within the Labour movement. Indeed, in the late 1930s Callaghan (1987, p. 45) suggests that the party preferred to keep potential new recruits in the Labour Party to boost prospects for Communist affiliation and left unity campaigns. Such tactics helped reinforce Labour fears of Communist 'fellow travellers' within the party.

Yet the Labour and trade union leadership remained sternly resistent to both this persistent open courtship and the undercover infiltration by the Communists, who despite their converts among intellectuals, also made little real headway among the British working class. The Communists were a nuisance rather than a real threat, and certainly never a rival to Labour.

Moreover, despite the impressive intellectual support the Communist Party attracted, its doctrinal orthodoxy ensured that it produced little or nothing in the way of new political thought (Newton, 1969, ch. 2). In fact, some of the writers who joined the party seemed to have sought from it, not intellectual stimulation, but the kind of certainty and consolation that others have sought from religion, and it is perhaps no accident that some later turned from communism to Christianity.

Therefore, although there was a British Communist Party, there was not, until perhaps comparatively recently, a distinctively British communism. It is true that the party apparently endorsed the parliamentary road to socialism from 1951, but opponents were unimpressed, perhaps rightly in view of the British party leadership's endorsement of the Russian suppression of the Hungarian revolution of 1956, and their reluctance to accept the growing criticism of Stalinism which was beginning to emerge from Moscow itself. Hungary and disillusion with the Stalinist record did, however, lead to a considerable exodus from the party, and belatedly provoked some reappraisal among those who remained. In 1968, in sharp contrast with the earlier reaction to the invasion of Hungary, the Soviet invasion of Czechoslovakia was condemned. Following the example of some other western communist parties, notably the Italians, the British Communist Party moved away from their earlier slavish adherence to the Moscow line towards Euro-Communism.

The new approach was most clearly exemplified in the pages of the party's journal *Marxism Today*, which, under the editorship of Martin Jacques from the late 1970s onwards, showed a breadth far from doctrinaire, which was rare on the left and provided a major vehicle for the development of new analysis and ideas. It has been suggested that more fresh and stimulating analysis has come from the now tiny Communist Party than has emerged from the relatively hidebound and restricted Labour Party. Certainly, in 1989 the party produced a *Manifesto for New Times* which considered the implications of the far-reaching changes which had taken place in the

British economy and society, and which commanded respectful interest well outside the party's ranks.

Needless to say, the changes in the party have not been universally approved. Within the party, hardliners who still controlled the party's daily newspaper, the *Morning Star*, fought a strenuous rearguard action, despite the leadership backing for *Marxism Today*. On the left generally, some were suspicious of the new-found intellectual respectability and the surprising commercial success of the Communist Party's own theoretical journal, and there have been dark mutterings over 'designer Marxism'. More to the point perhaps, the party's new role as intellectual think-tank to the Labour movement is the corollary of its own political impotence, the end of former fantasies of the vanguard role in a British socialist revolution. The supreme irony is, however, that British Communism has jettisoned the narrow orthodoxies of Lenin and Stalin, and discovered a rich diversity in Marxist-inspired theory some fifty years too late, on the eve of the decisive repudiation of Soviet-style Communism over most of Eastern Europe, which threatens to discredit the whole Marxist intellectual tradition.

Trotskyism

The roots of British Trotskyism, of course, lie in Leon Trotsky's breach with Stalin, and his subsequent extensive critique of Stalinism. Trotsky's own early life as a charismatic revolutionary, his major role and independent stature in the Russian Revolution, his subsequent quarrel with Stalin, exile and eventual brutal murder by a Stalinist agent, would perhaps have been enough to ensure his sanctification by Communist sympathisers who felt that the Russian Revolution had somehow gone wrong. However, his own lucid writing, coupled with the brilliant advocacy of his biographer Isaac Deutscher, have helped to preserve the Trotsky cult long after his death. Trotsky has continued to provide inspiration for those revolutionary socialists, who have rejected the example of Stalinist and post-Stalinist Russia. In Britain there is not just one, but several distinct brands of Trotskyism, embodied in different groups and parties on the far left.

As Callaghan (1987) points out, however, Trotskyism has been as narrow and doctrinaire an ideology as orthodox communism.

Trotsky, while repudiating Stalin, endorsed Lenin, who had, before his own death, already effectively established an authoritarian political system which stifled dissent. Hence, Trotskyism generally involved the uncritical acceptance of Leninism, and some of the British Trotskyist groups showed a dogmatic doctrinal orthodoxy which rejected any deviation from the true Leninist faith as heresy.

The most dogmatic of the British strands of Trotskyism was displayed by the various groups dominated by Gerry Healy from the late 1940s through to the 1980s, including particularly the Socialist Labour League (SLL) and the Workers' Revolutionary Party. Any who challenged Healy's own line and his supremacy were expelled, in periodic purges. Some success was enjoyed in pursuing entryist tactics towards the Labour Party, but according to Callaghan (1987, p. 80) the SLL was already declining when the ambitious decision to turn it into an independent political party was taken in 1973. Repeated forecasts of the imminent collapse of capitalism were invalidated by events, and the party finally collapsed into division and disarray, amid charges of sexual misbehaviour by its septuagenarian leader which provided a field day for the popular press.

More intellectually respectable and less exclusive variants of Trotskyism were the International Socialists, who were transformed after 1977 into the Socialist Workers' Party and who put their faith in growing trade union militancy, and the relatively small International Marxist Group, which was particularly influential among academics and students. Both had some success in exploiting industrial disputes and single-issue campaigns, such as CND, Vietnam and Northern Ireland, but both, despite their proletarian rhetoric, made relatively little impression on the industrial working class.

The Trotskyist group which has achieved the greatest media attention, and a degree of notoriety, is none of the above, but Ted Grant's Revolutionary Socialist League, and, more particularly, the newspaper *Militant* founded in 1964, which officially has no relationship with its parent organisation although the links have been clearly established (Callaghan, 1987, p. 196). Relying on the fiction that there is no organisation behind *Militant* and that it is just a loose network of newspaper promoters and sellers, the Militant Tendency has been successful in dominating the Labour Party Young Socialists, and infiltrating a number of Labour constituency parties, leading to the selection of Militant-backed Labour Party parliamentary candidates, and the virtual takeover of the Liverpool Labour group. Alarm within the Labour Party coupled with adverse media publicity led to the expulsion first of *Militant*'s editorial board, then of members suspected of Militant connections both in Liverpool and elsewhere. The expulsions still leave Militant with several Labour MPs, although the general feeling seems to be that the influence of the Tendency is on the wane.

Doctrinally, the Militant Tendency is dogmatic, narrow, and particularly resistent to new currents of thought on the left. To this extent, Militant has shown little interest in feminism, ethnic minorities, local economic development, or decentralisation; and, to judge by the Liverpool experience, their approach in office is akin to old-style municipal socialism or labourism, with the emphasis on mass housing, bureaucratically administered, as the main solution to the problem of urban decay.

The future of Trotskyism in any form as a distinct strand of political thinking now seems problematic. International developments, particularly the changes in Russia and Eastern Europe, would seem to threaten its viability. Significantly, the repudiation of Stalin and authoritarian dictatorship has not led to a rehabilitation of Trotsky, who, in the context of the democratic movement, seems an irrelevant figure in the east. Logically, this would seem to indicate that Trotskyism as it has been practised since the 1930s has no future in the west either, but Trotskyist groups have been adept in the past in explaining the renewed relevance of their creed in altered circumstances, and in detecting propitious signs of revolutionary potential in superficially unpromising situations. No doubt their intellectual ingenuity will be sufficient to sustain a small but limited following, and replenish defections through new converts.

The far left and the Labour left

It has not been possible in this discussion of the far left to avoid frequent reference to the Labour Party, itself an indication of the essential weakness of the non-Labour left. Unlike many socialist parties on the continent, Labour did not split into separate revolutionary and reformist parties in the 1920s, and subsequent defections, such as that of the Independent Labour Party in 1932, have only served to show how difficult it is for a non-Labour socialist party to survive in Britain. Socialists have therefore frequently had to choose between compromising their ideals and aspirations by working within the broad Labour coalition, or preserving their ideological purity in fighting for one of a variety of forlorn prospects outside it. Some have oscillated between these alternatives, depending on the prospects for the left within the Labour Party. At times, such as the early 1960s, 1970s and 1980s, the Labour Party appeared to be moving decisively towards the left, and attracted unattached socialists as well as deliberate infiltrators. At other times, for example, during the later 1960s and the later 1970s, some socialists gave up Labour in despair, and joined non-Labour socialist groups and parties, or devoted their energies to single-issue campaigns.

For many socialists the question of whether to work in or outside, through or against, the Labour Party is essentially tactical. Most of the left socialist strands of thought which can be found outside the Labour Party can also be found inside it. Some of these strands are inconsistent with Labour's general commitment to parliamentarism and constitutionalism, and from time to time the Labour leadership has been sufficiently concerned to mount purges and expulsions. At other times, the party has been content to enlist their energies and turn a blind eye to their heresies. Revolutionary socialist groups themselves have alternated between strategies of undercover infiltration and open competition.

The far right

If there has been little scope for the far left outside the Labour Party, there has arguably been even less scope for the far right outside the Conservative Party. This partly reflects Conservative success in containing potential splits or defections, and partly the familiar, and of course not unconnected point, about the strength of the prevailing political culture, with its commitment to parliamentarism and moderation. As with the Labour Party, there were periodic howls of anguish from Conservatives at betrayals by the leadership – for example in 1832 over parliamentary reform, in 1846 over Corn Law repeal, in 1911 over curbing the power of the Lords, and in 1956 over the retreat from Suez. But the 'diehards' rarely persisted with their opposition, and in any case, there was nowhere else to go. More significantly, there were few of the conditions which supported far-right movements in other countries. Thus, after the decline of Jacobitism in the eighteenth century, there were no supporters of dispossessed regimes to provide a focus for right wing opposition – no monarchist party. Nor were there dispossessed aristocrats or great landowners thirsting for revenge against the liberal bourgeoisie, nor a substantial rural peasantry opposed to economic and social change. There was no sizeable professional standing army which might have provided the source and potential muscle for right-wing disaffection. For the nineteenth and first half of the twentieth centuries a degree of complacency about Britain's great power status reduced the scope for the kind of fanatical assertive right-wing nationalism which seems to have been fed in some countries by defeat and humiliation. Even the dismantling of the British empire, although it provoked some anger and dismay on the right, was relatively peaceful, and did not lead to a substantial influx of former settlers, angry and bitter at their dispossession and betrayal, to form the nucleus of a far-right opposition.

Britain never had flourishing right-wing nationalist, legitimist, agrarian, religious, or simply reactionary parties. Cynics might argue that they were hardly needed, as all these tendencies could be contained within the Conservative Party. Although there is perhaps some truth in this, it is also the case that the Conservative Party has only survived and thrived because it has never allowed itself for long to be dominated by a particular right-wing tendency or reactionary faction.

Right-wing groups, such as the League of Empire Loyalists in the 1950s, and more recently the Monday Club, have operated on the fringes of the party, but have either not sought, or not obtained, substantial popular support. On the other hand, disaffected Conservative politicians have sometimes attracted an extra-parliamentary following, but this has rarely if ever been translated into an organisational form which could challenge the party. The only real far-right alternative to Conservatism which has been presented to the British electorate is some brand of fascism, or quasi-fascism.

Fascism

Most European countries between the wars experienced strong fascist or quasi-fascist movements, and in some there have been distinct echoes of fascism in the post-war era. In Britain, fascist and overtly racist political parties have had relatively little impact. Mosley's British Union of Fascists attracted considerable publicity in the early 1930s, but never posed a serious threat, and was in manifest decline well before the Second World War. In the post-war period, although Mosley himself made spasmodic attempts at a political comeback, it was a new party, the National Front, which inherited his constituency, and his appeal, based on a mix of patriotism, racism and violence, but which was even less successful.

Fascism was always a rather strange amalgam of ideas, and it is perhaps easier to describe what it was against rather than what is was for. Essentially a product of the twentieth century, fascism was a comparative latecomer to the political scene, and, to a degree, involved a reaction against earlier political beliefs and ideologies. 'The essential anti-character of its ideology and appeal' (Linz, in Laqueur, 1979, p. 15) has been widely noted. Fascism certainly can be seen as a reaction against the rationalism, individualism, liberalism, parliamentarism and democracy which constituted the mainstream West European and British political tradition. Other antagonisms implied strange contradictions, which were part of the essence of fascism. To an extent it involved a reaction against industrialisation and urbanisation, and the whole modern world. At the same time, fascism was clearly a product of that same modern world, and fascist leaders proved adroit at exploiting modern methods of communication, using twentieth-century technology to promote traditional symbols and values. Fascist and Nazi government involved the same strange blend of traditional values and modern technology.

Fascism also managed, remarkably, to be both revolutionary and reactionary, anti-bourgeois and anti-communist. One influence was the anti-democratic and anti-Marxist elitism of Pareto and Michels. From the start, fascists were virulently anti-communist, and assisted in strike-breaking, an activity which attracted financial and other backing from industrialists. But both fascism and Nazism also involved anti-capitalist socialist rhetoric, drawing particularly on anarcho-syndicalist ideas, and it was this apparently revolutionary social programme which appealed to at least a sizeable minority of industrial workers in Italy and Germany.

For some, fascism promised a middle way between communism and capitalism – a new economic and social order which would transcend old divisions. Instead of class conflict and dissension it offered unity, order and discipline. There were elements in fascism which could appeal to the idealism of the young, and those disenchanted with the messy compromises, wheeling and dealing associated with old-style parliamentary politics. Corporatist ideas, as developed by Mussolini in Italy, were seen as the antithesis of parliamentarism, party political games, and industrial conflict. Yet at the same time, the other face of fascism, the glorification of physical force, and the use of violence and intimidation, were present from the beginning. Other omnipresent features were of course the cult of leadership, authority and quasi-military organisation, extreme nationalism and racism.

Some commentators have sought to differentiate between fascism in opposition and fascism in power, between fascism and Nazism (Sterhell, in Laqueur, 1979, pp. 328–9), and between fascist movements in different countries and continents. Even so, there remains a fairly strong family resemblance between all these various manifestations of fascism. In the case of Britain, Mussolini's original model was fairly faithfully imitated, both by his various admirers in the 1920s and by Mosley's British Union of Fascists in its early years. Later, Nazism, with its greater emphasis on anti-Semitism and biological racism, became a more potent influence.

It is difficult to interpret fascist ideology wholly or substantially in terms of class interests (Mercer, in Donald and Hall, 1986), although some Marxists have interpreted it as the product and rationalisation of a particular phase of capitalism. In fact, fascism seems to have drawn some support from a wide range of classes and groups within society – from traditional elite groups, from the middle classes, from both industrial and industrial workers, and from intellectuals. Some interpretations draw on psychology rather than sociology – for example, fascist sympathies are related to patterns of upbringing and an 'authoritarian personality'. The notion seems inherently plausible, and suggests the possibility of relating other ideologies to personality. Even so, its explanatory potential appears limited, as it fails to demonstrate why fascism flourished in some countries and made little impact on others. Political explanations rather than socio-economic or psychological explanations seem to have most mileage in them. Thus, fascism flourished in countries which suffered military defeat, national humiliation, political instability and recurrent political crises. The relative absence of such factors in Britain is a partial explanation of the relative weakness of British fascism.

Nevertheless, interest in, and support for, fascist ideas was far from negligible in Britain in the 1920s and early 1930s. It was the supposedly more positive aspects of Mussolini's fascism – economic progress, corporatism, order and discipline which aroused some respectful attention in British establishment circles. The less savoury aspects of his regime (which did not then include anti-Semitism) were played down or ignored. There were, however, some native nationalist and racist groups which responded more enthusiastically to fascism. A British Fascist group was established as early as 1923, in direct emulation of Mussolini's example, and this moved from anti-communism and strike-breaking to a full fascist programme by 1930. There were also a number of right-wing anti-communist nationalist groups with quasi-fascist ideas, including the British Empire Union, the National Citizens' Union, and some smaller breakaway fascist movements, such as the National Fascisti, and the Imperial Fascist League, the last of which was strongly anti-Semitic (Benewick, 1972, ch. 2; Thurlow, 1986, ch. 3).

It was, however, none of these, but Oswald Mosley's British Union of Fascists, founded in 1932, which came to be seen as the embodiment of British fascism, and either absorbed or rendered irrelevant other groups. Mosley himself had some claims to be regarded as a heavyweight politician and thinker, but although he clearly possessed some charisma, his intellectual qualities and originality have perhaps been exaggerated. He had been an apparently fairly successful mainstream party politician, but he was never entirely comfortable within conventional parliamentary politics. He had begun his career as a Conservative MP. Then, after a brief spell as an independent, he had transferred his allegiance to Labour, going on to become a minister in Macdonald's 1929 Labour government. When his quasi-Keynesian ideas for fighting unemployment were rejected by the Government, and then, more narrowly, by the Labour Party, he resigned, and went on to form his own New Party, with some support and wider sympathy from MPs, prominent figures and intellectuals across the political spectrum. Defeat in 1931 in by-elections and the General Election turned Mosley rapidly away from conventional parliamentary politics towards a fascist ideology, closely modelled on Mussolini's example (Benewick,

1972, ch. 7), and the New Party was soon converted into the British Union of Fascists (Benewick, 1972, ch. 3).

In the process Mosley lost most of his early respectable political and intellectual support. Partly, perhaps, in compensation, he increasingly exploited anti-Semitism in poor working-class areas, notably the East End of London (Benewick, 1972, p. 152; Thurlow, 1986, pp. 104ff.). Anti-Semitism was derived more from Nazism than fascism, and rapidly, along with virulent nationalism and violence, became central to Mosley's appeal. This, however, was already fading by the late 1930s, as his movement's models and exemplars appeared increasingly a threat to Britain's interests (Carsten, 1967, p. 222). After a spell of internment during the war (Thurlow, 1986, ch. 9), Mosley re-emerged to set up a new organisation in 1948, the Union Movement, with a remoulded 'Euro-fascist' ideology (Taylor, 1982, p. 8). He drew some support from the same London East End areas where he had been popular before the war, yet his involvement in British politics became increasingly sporadic. Although he attempted to exploit hostility to immigration in the 1950s and early 1960s, it was new far-right groups with new leaders which then secured some publicity and support for racist programmes.

The most significant of these new groupings was the National Front, itself the result of a merger between two earlier bodies, the League of Empire Loyalists and the British National Party (Thurlow, 1986, p. 278). Whereas Mosley had openly proclaimed his fascist beliefs, some of the post-war extreme-right groups and leaders were more cautious in admitting fascist sympathies. The National Front certainly included supporters and even leading figures whose nationalism and racism did not necessarily extend to a full acceptance of or even acquaintance with fascist or Nazi ideology. But some of its more prominent figures had clear Nazi associations (and Nazism was perhaps now a more significant influence than fascism, in so far as the two creeds can be effectively distinguished). Taylor (1982, p. 77) claims that the National Front ideology corresponded closely with the ideas in Hitler's *Mein Kampf*, and details thirteen common features. He goes on to suggest, however, that the National Front restricted its full fascist or Nazi ideology to an 'inner circle' of 'insiders', while resting its more general populist appeal substantially to the race and immigration issue.

The National Front for a time successfully exploited racial tension and opposition to immigration, achieving some media prominence and even, apparently, electoral support. It secured 16 per cent of the total vote in a parliamentary by-election in West Bromwich in 1973 and comparable support in a handful of local government wards located in areas of high immigration in 1973 and again in 1977. But the fears which such performances aroused proved exaggerated. The Front never managed to elect a single councillor, averaged only 3 per cent per candidate in the 50 or so seats fought in the General Elections of 1974, and received a humiliating 1·3 per cent of the vote when it ambitiously contested over three hundred seats in 1979 (Taylor, 1982). Since then it has managed to survive, but appears a spent force.

The failure of British fascism to make a bigger impact may be variously explained. Benewick (1972) attributes Mosley's failure largely to the moderation, constitutionalism and parliamentarism of British political culture and tradition. Taylor (1982, pp. 179–80) similarly suggests the failure of the National Front could be attributed to 'resistance of the English to extremism' and an English 'commitment to moderation and democracy'. There is clearly something in this. Liberal democratic institutions and values were far earlier and more firmly established in Britain than in Italy, Germany, Spain, Eastern Europe or even France, where fascist ideas had a more ready reception.

Yet perhaps one should not be too complacent about any inherent inconsistency between British political culture and fascism. Fascist movements achieved most support in countries which had suffered military defeat or national humiliation. In some cases fascist ideas flourished only in direct response to occupation and external pressure. A British defeat in 1940 would have produced the same pressures for collaboration, and the same encouragement for fascist and Nazi ideas as occurred in other occupied countries. The opposite happened in Britain. While earlier, fascism had considerable appeal for extreme nationalists, increasingly, British patriotism seemed incompatible with fascism and Nazism. Hitler and Mussolini became figures of hatred and derision, and open espousal of Nazi symbols appeared treasonable. In the event, the National Front made some headway while it confined itself (in public as least) to exploiting racist and anti-immigrant feelings, but the firm identification of the National Front with Nazism – 'The National Front is a Nazi Front' – perhaps helped erode support (Taylor, 1982, p. 138).

While Britain has not been receptive to fascism, explicit or implicit racism has been widespread, and has been given some support by mainstream politicians and parties, who have pandered to popular opposition to immigration in general from the turn of the century onwards, and to 'coloured immigration' in particular after the Second World War. In the latter case, it was the speeches of Enoch Powell in 1968, then a Conservative shadow spokesman, and a former minister and challenger for the party leadership, which helped dramatise the immigration issue, and gave it political respectability (Taylor, 1982, p. 20). It was Mrs Thatcher who appeared to give some legitimacy to hostility to immigration, with her celebrated reference to fears of being 'swamped' (Taylor, 1982, p. 144). One explanation, therefore, for the decline of the National Front is simply that their natural constituency has been eroded by tough anti-immigration government policy, and the appeasement of racism (Layton-Henry and Rich, 1986).

7

Beyond Left and Right: New Directions in British Politics

Introduction

All the political ideologies so far considered can be fairly easily placed on a conventional left/right political spectrum. They can also be readily located between the 'two contrasting extremes of libertarianism and collectivism' in terms of which Greenleaf (1983, Vol. I, p. 14) suggests that 'modern British politics may be portrayed', or on a similar scale of 'attitudes towards the modern state' as indicated by Barker (1978, p. 5). With rather more difficulty and some considerable qualifications, all of them can be related to class interests, although of course, the legitimacy of such an exercise would not always be recognised by the adherents of a particular ideology.

Yet there are significant currents of thought in modern British politics which cannot be easily categorised as 'left' or 'right', 'libertarian' or 'collectivist', pro-state or anti-state, and which cannot be readily related to social-class interests. Indeed they involve, ostensibly at least, quite different categories of analysis, which cut across class or render it irrelevant. Among such currents of thought may be included nationalism, political movements relating to ethnicity or religion, feminism, and environmentalism.

It may be objected that these are not distinctive political ideologies in the traditional meaning of the term. Some may be regarded as derivative from mainstream ideologies. So, nationalism may be seen as an aspect of conservatism or fascism, rather than as a separate ideology, while feminism may be seen as an application of liberal or socialist principles. Partly, this is a matter of perspective. For some, such questions are essentially secondary and subordinate, but for others the issue of nationality, or gender, or religion, or the environment, seems central to their whole way of viewing the world, and the main spur for political activity. These perspectives involve distinctive ideologies which should be subjected to the same critical analysis as socialism, liberalism and conservatism.

In practice, although there is a substantial specialist literature on feminism, and a fast-growing literature on environmentalism, largely written by and for Greens, these perspectives are relatively neglected in most of the existing general literature on British political ideas. Feminism, ecology and environmentalism do not appear in the index of Greenleaf's (1983) massive work on Britain's ideological heritage, and even nationalism only receives a passing mention. They are similarly ignored in the second edition of Beer's (1982) influential account *Modern British Politics*. In both cases, the date of publication and the organising principle behind the books provide some excuse for the omissions, although Barker (1978) has some interesting things to say about feminism despite the fact that the same excuses would also apply. Feminism also receives a re-spectful mention in Eccleshall's introduction to a jointly authored tome *Political Ideologies* (Eccleshall *et al.*, 1984), but, apart from some later brief discussion of socialist feminism, is subsequently ignored, although nationalism is accorded a separate chapter. A more recent similar collection, edited by Tivey and Wright (1989), perhaps precludes a serious examination of feminism by its emphasis on 'party' ideology, but also manages to ignore nationalists and the Greens totally, while paying extensive respectful treatment to social democracy.

The assumption here is that all these ideas are important in terms of modern British politics, and they are particularly worth examining precisely because they cut across much conventional political analysis. They raise disturbing questions about values, and categories and modes of analysis which compel some reassessment of traditional political thinking. Nationalism, for example, raises issues about allegiance and identity which many socialists might prefer not to face, but have to address. The Green movement and environmental concerns would seem to pose enormous problems for neo-liberalism, at the very time when that ideology has apparently re-established its hegemony (Hay, 1988; Ashford, 1989). Political campaigns based on ethnic identity or religious conviction have all kinds of awkward implications for progressive liberalism and socialism. The notion of patriarchy is difficult for Marxists.

These ideologies are nevertheless important in their own right, and not just as sticks with which to beat conventional political analysis. They are not easy to explain and interpret on the same level as liberalism or conservatism, however. All of them involve values which transcend politics, and affect personal as well as overtly political behaviour. A green personal life-style may be regarded as more important than participation in Green pressure group activity or the Green Party. Some women may value the feminist message for its contribution to their own self-esteem, or for improving their relations with other women, rather than more clearly political implications. In so far as there are clear and acknowledged implications for political beliefs and behaviour, these do not necessarily find expression through a political party, as other mainstream political ideologies commonly do. Feminism is not generally linked with a specific political party at all. Environmental concerns have, more recently, been articulated by specialist Green parties, but this is by no means the only, or perhaps the most effective way that these concerns have been articulated, and in any case other political parties, with varying degrees of plausibility, can claim a concern over ecological issues. Nationalist sentiments do not necessarily involve supporting a political party which is clearly labelled 'Nationalist'.

It is also, of course, impossible to do justice to any of them within the brief confines of a single chapter. The organising principle under which they have been grouped together has been outlined above, but it has to be admitted that they have little in common beyond a resistance to conventional political analysis.

Nationalism

Nationalism is in general terms a fairly old political ideology, which immediately raises questions about its place in a chapter discussing new currents of political thinking. Even so, in the British political context, Welsh and Scottish nationalism are relatively new, and English nationalism, although in one sense very old, is a contested and difficult concept. Nationalism is thus part of a 'new politics', challenging the traditional political order and culture. It is necessary, however, to set the manifestation of nationalism in recent British politics in a broader historical context.

Although nationalist sentiments were clearly present in England in the sixteenth century, if not earlier, nationalism as a political doctrine dates from the late eighteenth or early nineteenth centuries (Kedourie, 1960, p. 9). It was closely associated in its early European form with liberalism. Self-determination for individuals and whole peoples were seen as complementary. Popular sovereignty entailed nationalism as well as democracy. Freedom from arbitrary or despotic rule frequently also involved freedom from foreign rule. Nationalism – the freedom of particular groups of people with a consciousness of a common identity to their own autonomous development – was seen as compatible with the free association of independent nations for their own mutual political and economic benefit.

Nationalist ideas almost from the beginning were also enlisted for conservative or reactionary purposes. Nationalist symbols were employed to secure the support and loyalty of subordinate groups in society for regimes serving a narrow class interest. Patriotism and imperialism were discovered to be potent weapons in weaning the industrial working class away from revolutionary demands. To the dismay of progressive liberals and socialists, national loyalties proved stronger than wider considerations. In the international sphere, a crude social Darwinism served to justify an aggressive, assertive nationalism which denied self-determination to others. The idealistic liberal nationalism of early nineteenth-century Germany and Italy did not lead to the new era of international peace, prosperity and co-operation foreseen by Mazzini (1805–72) or Bright, but to war, imperialism, and ultimately fascism. For these reasons, nationalism in the twentieth century came to be more commonly associated with the right of the political spectrum, with conservatism or fascism. Far from being regarded as a progressive force, it was commonly viewed as reactionary, and even pernicious.

At the same time, on a world scale, nationalism could be identified with the anti-colonial struggles of peoples in other continents against the western imperial powers. This kind of nationalism seemed particularly compatible with socialism, and fitted neatly within Lenin's analysis of capitalist development. Accordingly, nationalist movements, in this context, could still be seen as popular and progressive, and part of a world-wide struggle for the liberation of the poor and oppressed. In practice, many third world nationalist movements were also socialist or explicitly Marxist.

Yet the strength of nationalist loyalties has continued to embarrass both liberals and socialists.some newly independent former colonies have proved almost as aggressively nationalist as the products of nineteenth-century nationalism. In Eastern Europe and the Middle East, nationalism has often seemed a more potent force than either socialism or liberal democracy.

A narrow nationalism is difficult to explain or justify within a liberal or socialist ideology. For the liberal, nationalism is based on the principle of self-determination, and the nation ultimately exists to serve the interests of the individuals who compose it. National interests cannot be invoked to justify interference with fundamental individual rights. Liberals have faced considerable conscientious scruples on the issue of conscription, for example. National interests in the economic sphere may cut across the principle of free trade.

For the socialist, liberal individualism is based on a fundamental misconception. Man is a social animal, shaped by social forces. The nation state, however, was seen as the product of a particular stage of capitalist development. The crucial divisions in society were along lines of economic interests, and national loyalties were artificially fostered rather than natural. While nationalist movements might be supported by socialists where they appeared to be allied to progressive forces, ultimately national loyalties conflict with class and humanitarian loyalties. As Hobsbawm (1989, p. 125) tartly observes 'any Marxists who are not, at least in theory, prepared to see the "interests" of their own country or people subordinated to wider interests, had best reconsider their ideological loyalties.'

To the conservative, nationalism presents fewer difficulties. In the early nineteenth century the doctrine had disquieting revolutionary implications for conservatives (Minogue, 1967). The concept of the nation was invoked against the state, the people against established government. Yet subsequently state and nation were conflated, and nationalism or patriotism could be seen as the cement of social

authority, rather than potentially subversive. To the modern conservative, nationalism is both natural and healthy. The nation is but
one, although the most important, of a hierarchy of natural associations in which people are bound by ties of mutual obligation and
dependence. The nation is logically prior to the individual, who
owes allegiance to it.

Nationalism in Britain

As far as nineteenth-century Britain was concerned, nationalism
was essentially a principle to apply to other countries, to Greece,
Italy, Germany, Poland and Hungary, for example. Its application
to Ireland was rather more controversial, although the question of
Scotland and Wales was then largely unproblematic. Support for
nationalist movements in Europe were deemed quite compatible
with imperialism – the white man's burden. It rarely seems to have
occurred to even liberal progressive Victorians that the claims of
Arabs or Indians to self-government were on the same level as those
of Greeks, Italians or Poles.

If nationalist doctrine was regarded as irrelevant as far as Britain
was concerned, the allied concept of patriotism raised fewer awkward questions. Patriotism was not originally linked closely with
conservatism. Patriotic sentiment was associated with opposition to
the government in the eighteenth century, and was not a very
significant Tory or Conservative theme in the early nineteenth century (Cunningham, in Donald and Hall, 1986, ch. 11). In the later
nineteenth century liberal support for foreign nationalist movements and international ideals helped Disraeli to hijack the symbols
of British patriotism and imperialism for the Conservative Party.
From then on, British nationalism and Conservatism have been
closely identified, although the precise form of that nationalism has
been differently expressed and subtly redefined to meet changing
circumstances by, among others, Baldwin, Churchill and, most recently, Mrs Thatcher (Schwarz, in Donald and Hall, 1986, ch. 12).
Conservative nationalism seems to have reaped considerable electoral dividends, tapping a rich seam of patriotism or chauvinism
among the British working classes. Such sentiments have been
sufficiently potent to shape Labour politics also, although 'little
Englander' Labourism has not been sufficient to prevent the party

from being periodically branded as 'unpatriotic' by its Conservative opponents.

But if British national sentiment is clearly potent, and a significant influence on domestic politics, it is by no means clear exactly what British nationalism now involves. There is first of all the ambiguous relationship of British and English nationalism. For the majority of English the two terms are virtually interchangeable, but not, clearly, for Scots or Welsh. Then there is the question of the British empire, once a powerful unifying symbol, and a source of employment and potential personal prosperity for Scots, Welsh and English, but now virtually defunct. For some on the extreme right, the notion of a British race has been important. For others, culture and language are important attributes. But Britain has become visibly more cosmopolitan and multicultural in the post-war era, containing peoples whose first allegiance is not to England or Britain at all. At the same time it is involved in international and European associations which make national sovereignty an increasingly artificial concept, and nationalist attitudes outmoded.

One view is that the whole British state is no longer a viable entity, and may indeed break up quite soon (Nairn, 1981). Nairn suggests that the United Kingdom is not a modern nation state, but essentially resembles those outmoded ramshackle multinational states like the Austrian empire which, unable to contain modernising forces, eventually broke up. In this context, he sees Scottish and Welsh nationalism as essentially positive, progressive forces, assisting in the destruction of a virtually moribund British state.

Scottish and Welsh nationalism

Scottish and Welsh nationalism are both relatively recent, at least as political doctrines rather than sentiment. While Irish nationalism was clearly a significant political factor throughout the nineteenth century, most Scots and Welsh then seemed content with their participation within the United Kingdom, from which, it could be argued, they profited economically and politically. In the twentieth century, the established British parties have all, to varying degrees, paid some regard to national sentiment, establishing separate national party organisations, and in government maintaining and strengthening the Scottish Office, and creating a Welsh Office. The

Liberals have been long committed to home rule for Scotland and Wales, while Labour became converted to devolution, involving separate directly-elected assemblies for Scotland and Wales from 1974. This, however, could be seen as both a reaction to the growing nationalist tide in Scotland and Wales, and insufficient to satisfy nationalist aspirations, which now, for at least a substantial minority, involved full independence.

Substantial support for nationalism, in the sense of full independence for Scotland and Wales, is very recent. The Scottish National Party (SNP) and Plaid Cymru were only founded in the 1930s, and neither achieved much electoral success before the late 1960s (Kellas, in Seldon, 1990), so that they are essentially modern political movements.

There are some interesting points of similarity and difference. The two parties have a common long-term objective, a common opponent, a common commitment to peaceful and electoral methods, and, of course, common ideological assumptions. Their growth has been roughly parallel, and the two parties have shown strong mutual sympathy and some practical co-operation.

At the same time, there are considerable differences between them. A familiar point is that while Welsh nationalism is essentially linguistic and cultural, Scottish nationalism is political and economic. The question of Welsh language and culture is central to Welsh nationalism, and gives it a depth of commitment and intensity lacking in Scotland, where the language issue is insignificant. But it also limits the appeal of Welsh nationalism largely to Welsh speakers. As Scotland is not divided by the language issue, the potential and actual support for nationalism there is greater. There is, moreover, a separate legal and educational system, and a far greater degree of administrative devolution, which provides a more substantial basis for a separate nation state. Economic arguments have also been more significant in Scotland. An early spur to Scottish nationalism was provided by the inter-war depression, with its catastrophic effect on Scottish industry. More recently, the discovery of North-Sea oil provided the prospect of an economically-prosperous independent Scotland. 'It's Scotland's oil' became a potent nationalist slogan.

There were also significant differences in the location of Scottish and Welsh nationalism on the political spectrum. Whereas Plaid Cymru was firmly associated with the left and socialism, a common gibe by Labour opponents of the SNP was that they were 'Tartan Tories'. The rapid growth of the SNP in the 1970s and the defection to it of erstwhile Labour supporters has weakened that charge, although it is still true that the SNP covers a wider range of views on domestic and economic policy than Plaid. But it is now easier for some socialists and Marxists to identify Scottish and Welsh nationalism with progressive neo-nationalism rather than the older reactionary nationalism of the nineteenth and early twentieth centuries. Nairn (1981) has argued persuasively that the 'break-up of Britain' is imminent, irresistible, and, from a socialist perspective, desirable. Hobsbawm (1989, ch. 10), by contrast, has vigorously denied that it is either inevitable or likely to advance the cause of socialism. In one sense, this can be seen as a private argument among Marxists, reflecting the old theoretical and practical problems of accommodating and explaining nationalism (Wright, in Tivey, 1981). It does, however, raise more general issues.

If nationalism does not reflect some form of crude social Darwinism, but a vision of the world divided up naturally into nation states, co-operating peacefully and harmoniously, this poses the question of what actually constitutes a nation, and how far in practice the process of national separation might go. Hobsbawm (1989, pp. 120ff.) suggests that requirements of political and economic viability for states in the nineteenth century provided some restraint then on political fragmentation or 'Balkanisation'. The development of an international economy on the one hand, and a balance of nuclear terror on the other, he argues, has rendered outmoded old assumptions about economic self-sufficiency and defence capability, and enabled tiny states to emerge and survive in the modern world. Thus, there is no practical brake on nationalist aspirations. The Basques or the Bretons, like the Scots and Welsh, can reasonably aspire to full sovereign independence. But if an independent Scotland, why not an independent Shetlands?

Others have suggested that a variety of modern developments have rendered the nation state an anachronism, eroded from above and below (Kolinsky, in Tivey, 1981). At one end, economic interdependence, and the participation of states in a whole range of international associations has transformed traditional concepts of national sovereignty. At the other end, pressures for participation and decentralisation have led in many countries (but significantly not Britain) to greater regional and local autonomy. Increasingly, it may appear that the old national-state level of government is but one in a hierarchy of authority. This does not, of course, necessarily weaken the case for Scottish or Welsh nationalism. Indeed, the emphasis on 'Scotland in Europe' explicitly links the demand for separation from England with full participation in Europe.

At bottom, nationalism is not primarily concerned with the optimum size of governmental units or considerations of administrative rationality, but with essentially subjective questions of association, identity and community. In this connection it is worth noting that strong loyalties may also be evinced for small localities, towns, cities and regions as well as nations. Whether natural or fostered, such loyalties, like nationalist loyalties, tend to cut across ordinary party political allegiances, and raise issues which transcend mainstream political ideologies. There has been an intermittent debate on local democracy and local autonomy in Britain for well over a century. Supporters and opponents of public intervention are to be found on both sides. To be anti-centralist is not necessarily to be anti-collectivist. At another level, the European ideal has had some minority but cross-party appeal. Arguments about local autonomy, nationalism and European integration may appear to have very little in common, but they all link political power with considerations of territory and community, rather than economic interest, and raise major questions which are relatively neglected in mainstream ideological debates.

Race and ethnicity

Nationalism is almost inevitably exclusive in its appeal. While it may appear to include anyone who happens to be living in the territory claimed by nationalists as their own, in practice some more positive connection with the nation is required. Recent English settlers in Wales are unlikely to be regarded by their neighbours as Welsh, nor potential recruits to Plaid Cymru. Residence over a period may secure formal citizenship in some independent states, although others, like the United States, may additionally require the passing of tests. Yet formal citizenship, even sometimes of long standing, is not always sufficient to gain acceptance by fellow nationals. Some versions of nationalism have effectively denied that it is possible for certain groups to belong. Extreme German, French and Polish nationalists, for example, have denied that a Jew can be a member of their nation, while the National Front would reject the very concept of 'black Britons'.

Race is a problematic and sensitive concept. The purportedly scientific theories of racial differences advanced by the Nazis have, of course, long been discredited. Still, broad distinctions of ethnic origins are manifest, have received some official recognition for purposes of classification and monitoring of discrimination, and may also be a matter of subjective acknowledgement and pride. Britain, in common with many other countries, now contains peoples from many different ethnic backgrounds, and significant ethnic minorities, particularly following substantial immigration in the post-war period from what is euphemistically called the New Commonwealth.

The early assumption of most liberals, and perhaps the bulk of the immigrants themselves, was that the end product should be, and would be, total integration and assimilation within the host country, on the same pattern as earlier waves of immigrants such as the French Huguenots, or refugees from Eastern Europe. But skin colour alone made these immigrants and their descendants readily identifiable, and in practice they were targets for prejudice and discrimination by the native white population. Considerable racial tension and some overt racial conflict ensued.

The reaction of the British political establishment from the 1960s onwards was twofold – an increasing restriction on (effectively black) immigration, and race relations legislation to outlaw discrimination. The latter was not particularly effective, and was perhaps undermined by the racist nature of the immigration restrictions. Other aspects of the state's treatment of ethnic minorities also provoked criticism. The policing of the black communities in particular was felt to be prejudiced, discriminatory and oppressive, and aroused considerable hostility and alienation.

Those, particularly Afro-Caribbeans, who had initially wanted to integrate found they were unable to do so. They could not, apparently, however hard they tried, be treated as British or English, and this fostered, in reaction, a greater reliance on ethnic identity and consciousness. There were, of course, other immigrants, principally from the Indian sub-continent, who had never had any intention of submerging their own distinctive ethnic and religious identity within British culture.

For these reasons, assimilation and integration came to seem less feasible, and perhaps less desirable. The concept of a multicultural society, which accepted ethnic, cultural and religious diversity, was increasingly accepted by liberals and socialists, and by some conservatives, although the notion of a multicultural Britain posed some difficulty for traditional conservative nationalism. In general though, willingly or reluctantly, ethnic communities are now regarded as a fact of life and here to stay.

It is also clear that ethnic divisions have enduring potential and actual political implications. Even so, race and racism have been relatively neglected by British political scientists, both mainstream and Marxist (Solomos, 1986). Until recently, Marxists have tended to see both race and gender as subordinate to class. Racial prejudice and discrimination could be seen as a particular consequence of class domination and exploitation under capitalism. But some neo-Marxists now recognise that race cannot be treated simply as a subset of class, but is an important distinctive factor in politics (Dearlove and Saunders, 1984, p. 182).

Race is now manifest in British politics in a variety of ways. Some reference has already been made to white racism in the previous chapter. Although support for overtly racist parties seems to have declined recently, there are few grounds for supposing that racist sentiments have similarly declined, and it may be assumed that they will continue to be a factor in British politics in the foreseeable future. In opposition, anti-racist groups such as the Anti-Apartheid movement and the Anti-Nazi League have flourished and have had some success in countering racist or fascist movements. The hetero geneity of the ethnic minority groups themselves have inhibited the development of a common front. Thus, there is 'no common group identity or ideology which has been forged in their struggle with white society and finds expression in organised political activity' (Layton-Henry, 1984, p. 176). Indeed, there has sometimes been considerable hostility within and between ethnic minorities, spurred on occasion by 'homeland politics' (Jacobs, 1988, ch. 4). Such distant events as the Indian storming of the Sikh temple, the fortunes of Bhutto's Pakistan People's Party (PPP), and the invasion of Kuwait intensify existing ethnic, linguistic and religious divisions.

Electoral considerations, if nothing else, have forced the established parties to consider the implications of their policies for the ethnic vote. In general, the ethnic minorities themselves have been prepared to work with and through the existing political parties, particularly the Labour Party, although there has been increasing pressure for more recognition of their specific interests and the selection of black candidates for winnable seats. It has been clear for some time that the ethnic minorities are politically under-represented at every level, and under-represented, particularly in the higher levels, in public sector employment. There has been considerable pressure within the Labour Party for the establish-ment of separate black sections. Although this was resisted, the increased prominence of blacks in the party were a factor in secur-ing the election of four black Labour MPs in 1987, and increased representation in local government. This has had policy implications also, involving, for example, the widespread adoption of equal opportunities policies, coupled in some cases with effective monitor-ing. Greater susceptibility towards ethnic minority interests on matters of diet, clothing, language and religion have also been shown.

Such issues have provoked occasional incidents which have been exploited by racists, but have also sometimes raised awkward issues of principle for liberals and socialists. Deference to Muslim suscepti-bilities over the separate education of girls has sometimes appeared to conflict with a commitment to equal treatment for both sexes. Demands for separate Muslim schools, difficult to resist because of the acceptance of state-supported Catholic and other schools, raise fears of a racially segregated society. Full recognition of some demands, most notably for the banning of Salman Rushdie's book *The Satanic Verses*, conflicts with fundamental liberal ideas on free speech and toleration.

Religion

It is difficult here to disentangle ethnic and religious considerations. The Rushdie affair in particular has made religious belief a political issue in Britain in a way which it has not been since the seventeenth century. In the sixteenth and seventeenth centuries some people were prepared to die, and to kill, for what they conceived as the true religion. Subsequently, although religious discrimination and prejudice remained significant, and religious differences remained politically important throughout the eighteenth and nineteenth centuries, toleration of rival beliefs became a cardinal liberal principle. While historically Muslims can claim a far better record of toleration towards other religions than Christians, that toleration does not extend to attacks on what they regard as their own fundamental beliefs. Some appear to regard the publication of a book as deserving death, a not unfamiliar attitude in the religious wars of the sixteenth century in Western Europe, but a horrendous notion to the modern liberal.

The implications could go further. Religious affiliations have been of declining significance in twentieth-century politics in mainland Britain. Britain has never experienced explicitly Catholic, Protestant, or even Christian parties, of a type which have been common enough on the European continent. Ostensibly, religion has of course been a siginificant factor in the politics of Northern Ireland, but even with regard to that troubled province, the general political and academic consensus seems to be that the conflict is not essentially religious. However, not everyone agrees with this relegation of the role of religion in Northern Irish politics to a purely symbolic or superficial phenomenon (Bruce, 1987), and it may be that rational-minded political scientists are rather too reluctant to accept that religious convictions actually matter to some people.

Such religious convictions in Britain had clear political implications on single-issue campaigns, over, for example, abortion, sex education and censorship, but have not so far involved the development of a distinctive political ideology with far-reaching consequences for allegiance and behaviour. In the United States, evangelical and fundamentalist Christians have become an important factor in politics. A religious revival in Britain could have significant political implications. Muslim religious beliefs have already become a factor which politicians cannot ignore. In this context the establishment of an Islamic party is significant. To date, its impact has been minimal, but if it survives and flourishes it will represent, for Britain, a wholly new kind of religious-based political ideology.

A familiar point which used to be made about twentieth-century British politics was the extent of homogeneity (Jennings, 1966; Punnett, 1987). Only class differences were held to be particularly significant. Other cleavages – linguistic, cultural, religious, regional, ethnic – were considered relatively unimportant. In this way, British politics could be substantially explained in class or left/right terms, or in terms of associated ideological conflicts between individualism and collectivism. The politics of nationalism, ethnicity and religion have complicated the picture considerably.

Feminism

Similar points might be made about the politics of gender. The distinction between men and women is simple, fundamental and undeniable, and clearly cuts across other cleavages. Yet issues relating to gender have only attracted much political attention fairly recently, and are still widely viewed as peripheral. Feminists would suggest good reasons why this has been the case, and have also uncovered a substantial tradition of feminist thought, previously largely neglected by historians and political theorists (Rowbotham, 1973).

Feminism is clearly significant in modern British politics, although it is difficult and rather pointless to attempt to examine it in an exclusively British context. Feminism draws on a broad European tradition, and most modern feminist analysis in English is best described as Anglo-American. The application of feminist ideas will, however, be more specifically related to Britain.

What has become a fairly conventional classification distinguishes between liberal, socialist, and radical feminists (e.g. Charvet, 1982, introduction; Carter, 1988, ch. 7). To some degree it can be argued that really only the latter involves a distinctive ideology. Both liberal and socialist feminism can ultimately be seen as applications, if indeed very important and often neglected applications, of liberal and socialist principles.

British liberalism was indeed pretty slow to recognise women's rights among the individual rights it claimed to champion. While Mary Wollstonecraft's *Vindication of the Rights of Woman* (1792) is rightly regarded as a classic text of liberal feminism, it had little practical influence on mainstream politics or the liberal tradition. Arblaster (1984, p. 232) claims that 'liberals who championed women's rights, such as John Stuart Mill and his godson Bertrand Russell, stand out by virtue of their isolation.' Demands for female suffrage and full political representation, unanswerable on fundamental liberal principles, were not conceded by Asquith's Liberal government.

Even so, women's suffrage can be seen as the outcome and

expression of liberal feminism, and the same could be said of other legislation which has removed specific restrictions on women and attempted to place women on a footing of legal equality with men, particularly relatively recent measures to outlaw discrimination in employment, pay and taxation. By and large, legal and civil equality has been secured, and the gains for women should not be underestimated. There are few remaining legal bars to female advancement, and it is not difficult to find examples of women who have achieved positions of eminence in a wide range of fields.

At the same time, critics would suggest that the results of these endeavours also illustrate the limitations of liberal feminism. Legal equality between the sexes has not produced actual equality. Average female earnings lag well behind men's, despite equal pay legislation. Women are conspicuous by their rarity in the higher civil service, private sector management, and the upper reaches of the professions. Despite having the vote on equal terms with men for over half a century, women number less than 5 per cent of MPs and 20 per cent of local councillors. The important symbolic breakthrough of a woman prime minister has not seemingly advanced the position of women more generally. Indeed, liberal feminism has arguably enabled a small proportion of women to make spectacular progress in the professions and elsewhere, but has not had much impact on the opportunities for the bulk of women, effectively restricted to traditional female areas of employment, such as domestic, catering and cleaning work, retailing, low-grade clerical duties, and particular parts of manufacturing. It has been further suggested that the few successful professional career women are effectively dependent on the low-paid exploited labour of female 'dailies' and nannies. As a result, feminine liberation has only effectively benefited a small proportion of middle-class women. Liberal feminism involves a clear assertion of the equal rights of men and women, but does not provide any really coherent explanation for either the existence of male domination or the continuation of marked gender inequalities despite the achievement of legal equality. The only solution on offer is the removal of those loopholes in the law which apparently permit the perpetuation of discriminatory practices.

The label 'socialist feminism' is a broad one, covering early Owenist socialists, social democrats, and a variety of Marxist strands. In general, socialist feminists have laid more emphasis on the social conditioning which has led to an acceptance of male domination by both sexes. Gender inequality is linked to property relations in a capitalist society. Just as male wage labourers are necessarily exploited under capitalism, so the family, and women's role of unpaid domestic labour within the family, is required to support the male workforce. In this way, women are doubly exploited – as members of the working class, and within the family by men. The abolition of capitalist property relations would permit either the abolition of the family, or its transformation into an equal partnership. Either way, the more optimistic Marxist feminists suggest, the end of capitalism would entail the end of women's oppression by men.

More immediate objectives involve practical measures for the improvement of the conditions of all women, but particularly working-class women, through encouraging female involvement in trade unions, through the provision of nurseries and child-care and community services for elderly dependent relatives, through public transport, housing and social facilities, and through changes in taxes and benefits, perhaps including wages for housework. Recognition of the importance of social conditioning has led to attempts to control the role models offered to the public generally, but particularly to children, through gender stereotyping. Some of the more zealous attempts to eradicate sexism (as with similar measures on racism) have provoked ridicule from right-wing tabloid newspapers, but have also raised doubts among liberals.

Some socialist feminists have shown a particular concern over the physical exploitation of women, in terms of rape and other forms of violence both inside and outside marriage, and issues such as prostitution and pornography. The latter in particular involves some points of principle – should prostitution and pornography be banned as inherently degrading to women, or regulated to remove the more overt forms of exploitation, as liberals tend to argue? Those socialist feminists who favour banning sometimes find themselves uncomfortably in the same camp as those with a very traditional conception of women on the right of the political spectrum.

Violence against women is difficult to derive solely from the evils of capitalism, and some socialist feminists argue that female exploitation is not just a function of capitalism, but a more general feature of human society. Radical feminists tend to take this argument further. The problem is not an inadequate political and legal framework, as liberal feminists imply, nor capitalism, as socialist feminists suggest, but simply, men. Everywhere men exploit women. The central concept of radical feminists is patriarchy. To Kate Millett (1977) all known human societies have been and are patriarchies where women are controlled by men. Gender is the essential division in society, transcending in significance class, national, and ethnic divisions. Women themselves constitute an oppressed class. Male domination is the critical and universal form of power relations, creating an all-pervasive ideology.

Yet although patriarchy is a universal feature of past and present human society, radical feminists have not seen it as natural (or biological), but cultural, and ultimately capable of transformation. Proffered solutions have differed widely. One, advocated by some socialist feminists also, is abolition of the family. The family is viewed by most radical feminists as the principal institution for maintaining patriarchal society, hence its abolition is a necessary first step towards establishing equality between the sexes. For some, this does not go far enough. Women will not be free until they are liberated from the tyranny of their biology. Not only is child-rearing demeaning, but pregnancy barbaric, and ultimately may hopefully be replaced by artificial reproduction (Firestone, 1979).

Other radical feminists have moved in a quite different direction. They have rejected the liberal feminist goal of seeking equality with men, and minimising the essential differences between the sexes. Women's nature and behaviour is seen as different, and perhaps superior, to men's. Traditional feminine attributes are celebrated rather than spurned. Child-rearing may be seen as a means to fulfilment rather than subjugation, although it may not require the active involvement of men. Indeed, it can be viewed as an aspect of the caring co-operative nature of women, to be contrasted with the aggressive competitive behaviour of men. Far from competing with men, or seeking to ape them, women should be themselves. As for men, conceivably they might learn to become more like women, caring and compassionate, although there is some scepticism among radical feminists as to how far this transformation into a 'new man' is really feasible. Alternatively, women might be better off without men altogether, relying on their own mutual support. Significantly, while an early target of the women's liberation movement was male-only organisations such as Oxbridge colleges or London clubs, the development of exclusively female activities and associations among feminists has become common.

While the more extreme radical feminist ideas might attract ridicule or condemnation, not least among many women, radical feminism has also involved some acute analysis. For example, it has been suggested that some developments widely heralded at the time as an advance towards female liberation might have had the opposite effect. Easier sexual relations, aided by the greater availability and reliability of contraceptive techniques, and the legalisation of abortion, arguably produced more freedom for men than women, who were more open to pressure to submit to sexual demands. Easier divorce and increased family break-down left far more women heading one-parent families. Greater female employment opportunities in practice led for many, not to increased choice between a career and family, but a dual role of wage earner and major or sole domestic worker. Some of the leading feminist writers of the 1960s, such as Germaine Greer (1970), have pessimistically reassessed the objectives and achievements of that period, although it should also be said that not all feminists are happy with such revision.

Radical feminism, if widely adopted, would involve a completely different form of politics, with different principles, assumptions, analysis, priorities and policy proposals. Needless to say, that is most unlikely to occur. What is far more likely to happen is the continued permeation of conventional politics by feminist insights, a process which may not give much satisfaction to the women's movement.

The Greens and environmentalism

Ecology or environmentalism is the most recent of political ideologies, although there are, inevitably, antecedents. The Greens draw distantly upon such diverse strands as stoicism and pantheism, romanticism and the rediscovery of nature, Malthusianism, elements of anarchism, and even some aspects of fascism. Even so, the green ideology is essentially new. It has brought together a number of more specific concerns – over, for example, conservation, pollution, energy supply, population growth, safety, and animal rights – and woven these together into a coherent and distinctive ideology, which has become in a comparatively brief period re-markably influential over much of the world. The adoption of the colour green, fortunately not closely associated with any main-stream existing party or tendency in mainland Britain, has provided a powerful and readily identifiable symbol and image for the ecology movement the world over. People have little difficulty in identifying what 'the Greens' in essence stand for.

Yet, as with other ideologies, there are major differences of emphasis and internal divisions. Porritt and Winner (1988) refer to 'the astonishing diversity of political and philosophical views within the Green Movement', and go on to talk of 'the underlying tension between light green environmental reformism, and dark green holistic radicalism'. The latter includes 'gaianism' (after Gaia, the Greek goddess of the earth) or 'deep ecology' which perceives a spiritual relationship between man and nature, and regards the non-human world as of intrinsic value. Thus, human beings have no right to exploit the natural world, or other species within it.

Animal rights activists, who are prepared to threaten human life to counter the abuse of animals, provide an extreme illustration of such attitudes. Environmental reformists by contrast tend to assume the primacy of humanity and human values, and seek a wiser husban-dry of resources, and 'sustainable' rather than unlimited growth. Other distinctions include that between right-wing preservationists, and left-wing advocates of a radical alternative society – sometimes dubbed 'red-greens'. In countries like West Germany, where Greens have won significant parliamentary representation at both federal and state level, such fundamental differences have occasioned damaging public splits. This serves to emphasise how difficult it is to place the Greens on a conventional left/right political spectrum.

In Britain such differences have been less immediately apparent, largely because the Green Party has not enjoyed the levels of success of their German and other European equivalents. The biggest impact in Britain has been made, not by a political party, but by a range of environmentalist pressure groups, some well-established and respectable, such as the National Trust and the Council for the Protection of Rural England, and others more recent and radical, such as Friends of the Earth and Greenpeace. These have achieved substantial membership and support, and a formidable capacity to publicise environmental issues and force them onto the political agenda.

The Green Party, by contrast, has had negligible electoral success until recently. Formed in 1973 as the People Party, it was soon rechristened as the Ecology Party, and only changed its name to the Green Party in 1985 (Kemp and Wall, 1990). Although it has contested parliamentary and local elections since 1974, its progress was unspectacular, and it has normally struggled to secure more than one or two per cent of the vote. A major breakthrough was apparently quite suddenly achieved in the Euro-elections of 1989 with 15 per cent of the popular vote, a higher level of support than has been achieved by hitherto far more successful green parties on the European continent. Yet early indications are that the breakthrough has not been sustained. The Greens' reluctance to behave like a normal party, in, for example, the absence of a single leader, has perhaps hindered them from capitalising on their new-found popularity.

A familiar criticism, particularly from Conservatives, is that support for the Greens is not based on real understanding of their very radical programme, including opposition to nuclear weapons. Interestingly, some of the highest levels of electoral support were obtained in the Conservative south and south-east, indicating the potential for a split between radical activists and preservation-minded voters. This is the dilemma of the Greens everywhere. They can only secure mass support and effective political influence by advocating 'light green' reformist policies, and drawing on localist opposition to specific developments such as new motorways or high-speed rail links, or housing. Such accommodation and compromise with prevailing political values is at variance with more fundamental green ideas, and in any case can be pursued just as effectively by other established political parties.

And, of course, all political parties have attempted to jump upon the green bandwagon and claim a special affinity between a concern for the environment and their own ideology. Some liberals have long proclaimed green credentials, and indeed there has been pressure for electoral pacts, joint candidates and even merger with the Greens, although the saga of the Alliance and subsequent bungled merger with the Social Democrats perhaps precluded any serious accommodation. Within the Labour Party, while an interest in environmental matters has rarely in the past been displayed by trade unionists, revisionists, or the hard left, there have always been some socialists who have taken such issues seriously. A Socialist

Environmental and Resources Association (SERA) was founded in 1973, and ecology-minded socialists have achieved some significant shift in Labour policy, particularly over nuclear energy. Yet Labour and trade unionist commitments to the regeneration of British manufacturing industry and the expansion of employment, incomes and living standards runs counter to radical environmentalism, and reduces the prospect of any red–green alliance in Britain (Porritt and Winner, 1988, pp. 63ff.).

The conversion of the Conservatives under Mrs Thatcher to the green cause has been much trumpeted, although critics allege that it is an essentially cosmetic shift (Kemp and Wall, 1990, pp. 1–2). Conservatives can long claim to have had a special interest in the land, rural values and conservation, although the current New Right enthusiasm for the free market does not sit easily with the regulation and control which environmental protection requires. Even the National Front has taken up green issues (Porritt and Winner, 1988, p. 52), although the outrage of the greens at this apparently cynical political opportunism cannot conceal an uncomfortable affinity between fascist and Nazi rhetoric on a mystical bond of man with earth and soil (Pois, 1986) and the more fanatical adherents of gaianism and deep ecology.

Outside the mainstream party ideologies, it is often suggested that there is a close relationship between feminism and green ideas. Porritt and Winner (1988, p. 46) claim 'the convergence of interests between feminism and ecology has a long history', quoting Mary Wollstonecraft's nightmare vision of the future, nineteenth-century British feminist involvement in the anti-vivisection movement, and modern American eco-feminists. But as they also admit, there is 'a tension in the relationship between feminism and ecology', as 'nature is a loaded concept for feminists', pushing them into traditional passive and dependent roles. The 'earth mother' is a familiar feminine stereotype, although it is not an image which all feminists find helpful.

However, although all kinds of links can be found between the Greens and other political ideologies, environmentalism is, in the last resort, a very distinctive and perhaps unique political ideology. All the other ideologies so far examined can be linked to a particular social class or identifiable sectional interest, within society – for example, the working class, or women, or Muslims, or Scots. Now there are some who might link environmentalist concerns with such sectional interests. Elements on both the left and the right, for example, have suggested that preservationists are selfish well-heeled people concerned to protect their own property values and life-style against the aspiring or the poor. On a global scale, it is sometimes alleged that western concern with destruction of the Amazonian rain forests, or pollution in the third world, is a kind of neo-colonialism, designed to keep other countries poor and under-developed. Others would claim that the ecology movement is essentially a diversion from the real political struggle, a kind of late-twentieth-century 'opium of the people', dulling the senses on the critical questions of who gets what, how and when.

There is something in this latter charge, for if ecology is taken at its own valuation, the green ideology does seem different; in so far as it serves an interest at all, it is an interest which transcends present society and even perhaps humanity itself. It is concerned with generations yet unborn, with other species, and with the future of the planet. This poses a problem for conventional politics. There is no mechanism for taking into account the interests of future generations, still less, threatened flora and fauna, in either the economic or political market-place. Nor can the assumptions behind much traditional ideology accommodate such interests. Classical liberalism, with its assumption of enlightened individual self-interest, is able to take on board the postponement of present satisfaction for future pleasure, but scarcely its denial for the possible benefit to unknown future generations of human beings, let alone other species. Both evolutionary and Marxist forms of socialism assume progress towards higher living standards. The radical Greens require a collective sacrifice of current consumption and immediate aspirations on the part of humanity in the interests of an unknown and unknowable future. Such heroic unselfishness does not fit easily with the assumptions about humankind which are implicit or explicit in any mainstream western political ideology.

8

Retrospect and Prospect

The end of history?

Some thirty years after Daniel Bell announced the end of ideology, another writer has rather more ambitiously proclaimed the end of history (Fukuyama, 1990). On closer examination Fukuyama is celebrating not so much the end of history as the victory of one ideology. 'Liberal democracy is the only legitimate ideology left in the world.' Liberal democracy and 'the victory of market principles of economic organisation' are part of a universal trend sweeping the world, although he concedes that there are backwaters, like parts of the Middle East, which are still in the historical phase. Fukuyama's message is in one sense almost the opposite of Bell's. While Bell proclaimed the end of ideology, Fukuyama has celebrated the victory of ideas liberal democratic and free market ideas – over what he describes as 'realism', which he admits is still the dominant view among foreign policy professionals in Washington and Europe, and which 'maintains that conflict and competition are inherent in international politics'. Yet in another sense, both Bell and Fukuyama are making much the same point – ideological conflict is on the way out.

Fukuyama's views were published at an opportune time, when the disintegration of Soviet-style Communism in Russia and Eastern Europe heralded the end of the cold war. Dahrendorf (1990) has also discerned far-reaching ideological implications in the events of 1989. 'The point has to be made unequivocally that socialism is dead, and that none of its variants can be revived' (p. 38). While Dahrendorf is dismissive of Fukuyama's analysis, he too suggests that 'the old politics is spent' although he is less categorical and less complacent abut the future.

Britain has been far from immune from these intellectual tides. Indeed, on one flattering interpretation, Mrs Thatcher's vigorous championing of the free market has provided a significant model for Eastern Europe to emulate. Certainly, events there have been seized on by neo-liberals as providing significant confirmation of their analysis and prescriptions, while representatives of the New Right have been generous in proffering advice to the new regimes. Within Britain it has been suggested that the ideological polarisation following the breakdown of the old Keynesian consensus has now been replaced by a new Thatcherite consensus. Even the Labour Party, it is argued, has been finally obliged to abandon its socialist objectives and take on board essentially Thatcherite assumptions about the free market and competition.

However, this new assumption of ideological consensus seems no more firmly based than the last. Ignoring for the moment the question of socialism, there is a conflation of two perspectives, liberalism and conservatism, which still involve distinctive outlooks. Fukuyama seems to imagine that what he describes as 'realism' is a non-ideological perspective. Yet the world of 'realpolitik' or 'power politics', which suggests that aggression, competition and conflict are enduring aspects of the international scene, reflects a familiar conservative ideology, involving some fairly pessimistic assumptions about human nature and rationality, assumptions which have not been changed by the widespread emergence of liberal democratic regimes. The same doubts about human intellectual and moral capacities indeed impel conservatives to take a rather limited view of democracy itself. There is still a need for leadership, authority, and strong government, and only limited scope for popular participation in decision-making.

This conservative outlook is very different from post-Enlightenment optimistic rationalism which remains the essential liberal tradition. The tension between the two outlooks has been masked in part by an apparent liberal–conservative convergence in the ideas of the New Right and Thatcherism. Yet conservatives in Britain, Europe and the United States have only absorbed those economic aspects of liberalism which many liberals themselves over the last century have abandoned. Indeed, one reason why some conservatives have embraced part of the old liberal legacy, free market economics, is that it restricts the scope for radical democratic decision-making, which might threaten the interests of property. When it comes to the point, for conservatives the sanctity of property is paramount over liberal democratic principles, both in foreign and domestic policy. Thus, tensions between the liberal and conservative outlook, although masked by some confusion in ideological terminology, still exist and are likely to become more apparent as liberal principles and real interests diverge.

Fukuyama dismisses the threat to the liberal democratic order from national, ethnic and religious conflict, as aspects of the shrinking 'historical part' of a world moving inexorably towards the end of history. This seems optimistic at the least. Superficially, there appear to be an increasing proportion of the world's inhabitants whose political perspective is fundamentally informed by their membership of a particular nation or race, or their adhesion to a particular religion. At present, this is still a relatively small minority of the inhabitants of Britain, but it is growing.

Other distinctive ideological perspectives, such as radical feminism, and dark green environmentalism are ignored, yet both in their different ways involve a sharp challenge to the post-Enlightenment optimistic liberal rationalism celebrated by Fukuyama and others. Radical feminism draws attention to the violence done to women by men all over the world, and raises uncomfortable questions about the competitive and aggressive nature of man. Dark green environmentalism suggests the need for drastic action by governments and positive planning for the future, which cut across current neo-liberal assumptions. The philosophy runs sharply counter to the man-centred materialism of the post-Enlightenment liberal world.

Suggestions that ideological conflict is dead or dying seem no more convincing now than when they were articulated by Bell thirty years ago. If anything, the converse is true. Some of the perspectives which are now contesting for ideological supremacy transcend old divisions, and make the conflict of ideas far more complex. It is difficult to predict how current thinking on politics and society may evolve in the future, but ideological conflicts reflect divisions in society, and while divisions remain, ideological conflict will continue. Ideology is inseparable from politics.

Back to the future?

There is, however, still room for some speculation on how current political ideologies may evolve. It is, of course, possible that the future will closely resemble the past. Sometimes it appears that the evolution of ideologies involves the regular rediscovery and reinterpretation of the past, and the rehabilitation of past thinkers. For example, the present age has witnessed the rediscovery of the truths of classical economics, and the celebration in particular of the works of Adam Smith. As numerous commentators have pointed out, there is nothing new about the New Right, which involves the exhumation of ideas two centuries old.

This is not an isolated instance. Conservatism has often involved a harking back to a real or imagined past – Burke to an idealised revolutionary settlement, Disraeli to a quasi-feudal Merrie England of interdependence and mutual obligation, and many Conservatives since to an almost mythic Disraeli, whose reforming paternalism made one nation out of two. Conservatism inherently involves a reverence for the past, it might be suggested, but other political ideologies also draw inspiration from history. Scottish nationalists are attempting to recreate a separate Scottish state which disappeared nearly three centuries ago. Greens, for all their apparent modernity, express a vision of the future which sometimes looks disconcertingly like an idealised pre-industrial past. Even many socialists seem more interested in reinterpretations of Marx, and rediscovery of previously neglected or unpublished works, than in developing fresh analysis and solutions to meet modern circumstances.

What this seems to imply for the evolution of political ideologies is that the future is likely to bear a strong resemblance to the past. Ideas are likely to progress in circles – advanced, questioned, neglected and rediscovered. Originality will consist of the rehabilitation of forgotten thinkers and theories. The intellectual stock market will register some fluctuations in reputations over time, but there will be no crash or big bang. The underlying assumption is that there is nothing new under the sun.

Such an assumption should be questioned. Of course the past has to be understood to arrive at any understanding of the present. Of course important insights can be gained from the study of the past. Yet what all this pious genuflection to past ages and sages suggests is that they have the answers to the problems of the present and future, that there are important eternal truths lying around waiting to be rediscovered. Perhaps there are, athough it is important to recognise that this is an idealist conception. The alternative is to see ideas essentially grounded in the context of their time.

Adam Smith wrote in the eighteenth century in a Britain only on the verge of industrialisation. He could have no knowledge of a modern industrial society, posing problems which he could not have dreamed of. This does not necessarily invalidate his message, but it does indicate a degree of caution in applying his analysis and remedies to a very different society, two hundred years on. Marx similarly wrote in the middle of the nineteenth century. He can scarcely be accused of idealism himself; for Marx, of course, ideas were the product of history, the reflection of material circumstances. But if Marx were alive today, he would surely be somewhat puzzled by the way in which some of his latter-day followers have combed his writings for stray references to illuminate their understanding of the modern state, or bureaucracy, or nationalism, or the position of women. Marx, for all his insights, did not know the future, and it is hardly surprising that he underestimated some trends and failed to foresee others.

Excessive reverence for the wisdom of the past actually seems rather unhistorical. The political ideologies of today are mostly comparatively recent creations. The writers of the eighteenth-century Enlightenment speculated widely on politics and society, but had no acquaintance with the ideologies which have dominated the modern world. They may have contributed to liberalism, but would not have recognised the term and never saw it as a coherent ideology. They did not know or understand the doctrines of nationalism or socialism. They could scarcely begin to comprehend fascism.

This suggests the scarcely startling notion that liberalism or nationalism or socialism are not necessarily eternally valid (or invalid) truths, but the product of their time. They can all be seen as in some way related to industrialisation or industrial capitalism. What is also implied is that they may not always be around. Just as dramatic economic and social change in the early nineteenth century led to the appearance of essentially new political doctrines, so current or future economic developments may involve the virtual demise of some political creeds, and the appearance of other new doctrines, perhaps as unimaginable to us as fascism to the writers of the Enlightenment.

The question of the continued modern relevance of liberalism has already been alluded to (see Chapter 3). Some critics would argue that it is an ideology related to a particular phase of capitalist development, now past, and that liberalism is thus outmoded. Neo-liberals, by contrast, would point to the apparent triumph of free market ideas in the west, and the collapse of communist regimes in the east, and proclaim the death of socialism. This is not to suggest of course that either are necessarily right, merely that they could be.

Political ideologies are not immortal. Men fought over rival theories of the relationship between spiritual and temporal power in the Middle Ages, and where are those theories now? Nevertheless, it is difficult to envisage the eventual irrelevance of modern doctrines which have had such a potent hold over people's minds. Moreover, a degree of caution is in order when the failure of past prophecies are considered. Nationalism seems as vigorous as ever, despite repeated predictions of its decline. Few foresaw a revival of classical economics at the height of the Keynesian consensus. A capacity for adaptation and survival, however, is not a guarantee of eternal life. A world once existed without nationalism, and a world may yet arise where there will be no place for nationalist ideas. The future may not resemble the past.

A new world and new ideas?

There is no shortage of confident interpretations of current trends, or apocalyptic visions of the future, although these often appear, on closer examination, to involve more of a repudiation of the recent past. So, we have post-industrial society, or post-Fordism, or post-modernism, or post-capitalism. These influential pictures of the modern world tell us in some detail what we are losing, but only indicate sketchily where we are going. It is easier to characterise post-Fordist society by what it is not, rather than what it is. This is hardly surprising. It is difficult to recognise a trend when one is in the middle of it. Prediction is a chancy business, and some of the prophecies of our present futurologists may turn out to be ludicrously wide of the mark.

On the other hand, if some of these interpretations of current developments are anywhere near accurate, the implications for ideas could be considerable. The Industrial Revolution ushered in whole new ways of looking at the world. A post-industrial society, if it really involves change on the same kind of scale, could precipitate a similar revolution in ideas – the virtual disappearance of some hitherto influential doctrines, and the emergence of new, perhaps unimaginable creeds, as people try to make sense of their altered circumstances.

Of course, there are some fairly familiar older and also some more recently developed political ideologies which would claim a particular relevance for the future. Socialism was advanced by its early advocates as very much a creed of and for the future. Indeed, there are some socialists who would say that the problem with socialism, as others would observe of Christianity, is that it has never been tried (a view which raises awkward questions about the practicality of both creeds). Modern followers of Marx still antici-pate the eventual arrival of a socialist society, as the end product of developments now in progress.

In marked contrast, some have suggested that socialism is already dead. The rapid disintegration of Soviet-style Communism in East-ern Europe, and desperate attempts there to re-introduce a market-based economy suggest the total collapse of one form of socialism. Most British socialists would argue that they had never favoured this Russian model of socialism, and its collapse is to be broadly welcomed. It might either be regarded as totally irrelevant for British socialist prospects, or positively beneficial, in that it might facilitate the evolution of alternative forms of socialism. But the peoples of Eastern Europe seem to be repudiating not only Lenin-ism but any form of socialism. Furthermore, the highly publicised planning failures in Russia and Eastern Europe have reinforced the case of western advocates of the free market and critics of collectiv-ism. Even before the dramatic developments in Eastern Europe in 1989, the tide was running strongly against public ownership and state planning in Britain and most of Western Europe.

Others would posit that it is not the fashionability of certain ideas but economic and demographic trends which spell the death of social-ism. Socialism developed with industrialisation and the creation of a mass urban industrial proletariat. A post-industrial society, with a far smaller proportion of the population engaged in traditional large-scale manufacturing enterprises, will dramatically reduce the prospects for socialist parties everywhere. In Britain, the old working class is smaller and more divided. Natural trends have been exacerbated by deliberate Conservative government policy which has weakened and reduced the old natural Labour constituency of trade unionists and council house tenants. The working class is no longer so dependent on collective provision, and no longer has the same overwhelming interests in common.

It has already been admitted that political ideologies are not necessarily immortal, and it is quite possible that those who are already celebrating or regretting the end of socialism are right. But the announcement may be premature. Firstly, it seems probable that there will always be support for movements championing the interests of the poor and underprivileged and demanding some redistribution towards establishing a more equal society, and this is a necessary, although not perhaps a sufficient, condition for socialism. Secondly, a post-Fordist society seems unlikely to end all the pressures for government intervention which industrialisation produced. While some collective provision may be reduced, there are likely to be increasing pressures for state regulation and control on other grounds, particularly relating to energy conservation and the preservation of the environment. It also seems possible that problems with privatisation and currently fashionable market solutions may inspire some backlash in favour of increased planning. Finally, economic and demographic trends seem more significant for traditional British labourism than socialism. Socialism has not been tied everywhere to the existence of a large urban industrial working class. Socialism in Britain may therefore survive the decline of the specific class interest with which it has been associated, in the same way as conservatism survived the decline of the landed interest. However, it will involve considerable adaptation, and probably furious internal debates over whether whatever emerges is still socialism.

It would take a bold prophet to predict the end of British conservatism, which has been so conspicuously successful in adapting to changed circumstances in the past. There will clearly always be an ideology to reflect dominant interests in society, and conservatism, with its emphasis on leadership, authority, hierarchy and the sanctity of private property, is well placed to continue to fulfil that role. It is likely to continue to appeal to those opposed to high public expenditure and taxation, and irked by state regulations and controls. Patriotism and a strong line on law and order are conservative themes which seem probable to have a continuing popular appeal. Specific and general instances of antisocial and violent human behaviour may continue to confirm, for those of a conservative disposition, pessimistic assumptions about human nature, and reinforce demands for authority and discipline.

At the same time, some more recent themes, such as privatisation and the market generally, may be less emphasised. Privatisation has brought some short-term economic and electoral dividends, but the scope for further privatisation is not inexhaustible, and parts of the current and recent programme could present increasing political problems. If that happens, some modification of priorities and subtle restatement of conservative philosophy may appear necessary, but scarcely any fundamental rethinking, as a dogmatic attachment to the free market has not been a feature of conservatism historically. Traditional conservative caution in the face of change may be reaffirmed. Soft-pedalling the virtues of the free market may also help conservatives to be more convincing champions of the environment. Conservation issues of a light green variety clearly strike a strong chord with many traditional Conservative voters, and it is not one which the party can ignore.

Greens naturally believe that it is their analysis and remedies which have an urgent relevance in the transition to a post-industrial society. Perhaps, in retrospect, environmentalism will seem the ideology of post-capitalism, in the same way as liberalism or socialism may be seen as products of capitalism. Yet although green ideas and pressures have had a remarkable impact on British politics, up to the present this has involved only a modification of traditional political ideologies rather than the kind of total transformation of ideas and priorities which Green activists seek. Only a catastrophe, or a dramatic intensification of existing concerns on energy and food, seems likely to provoke serious general consideration of the radical change in life-styles and living standards which dark Greens believe is essential.

International rather than British political ideologies?

Environmentalism is an ideology which transcends national boundaries, and indeed, some of the other more recent developments in

British politics have a frame of reference which lies outside this country – the feminist movement, for example, or Islamic politics. Even Scottish and Welsh nationalism, which are necessarily particularist in their appeal, relate to international developments.

Mainstream British political ideologies are also becoming less parochial. Thatcherism has, uncharacteristically in the historical context of British conservatism, drawn inspiration from some non-British sources and examples, and it has been almost aggressively exported. Partly as a consequence, it has been closely associated with developments in other western countries and regarded as part of an international New Right phenomenon. The insular and idiosyncratic character of British conservatism may thus be undergoing some modification. However, it is still notable that British Conservatives have not found allies with whom to work among parties of the centre and right in the European Parliament, which suggests that their integration into the international mainstream should not be exaggerated. The Labour Party, apparently finally reconciled to membership of the European Community, has become rather more attuned to socialist ideas and practice in other western countries, while recent failures have provoked more interest in foreign experience. Hence, Labour's socialism may, too, be in the process of developing in a less insular and chauvinistic fashion.

It has been a major theme of and justification for this book that British political thinking is sufficiently distinctive to justify separate treatment, that there is a British socialism or liberalism or conservatism which requires relating to a specifically British context and experience. This certainly has been the case, and to a large extent still is the case. However, British political ideologies are becoming more closely related to wider currents of thought. If that is so, it may in the future be more difficult to justify a book substantially confined to the development and interpretation of specifically British political ideas.

Bibliography

Abrams, M., Rose, R. and Hinden, R. (1960), *Must Labour Lose?*, Penguin.

Adelman, P. (1970), *Gladstone, Disraeli and Later Victorian Politics*, Longman.

Adelman, P. (1986), *The Rise of the Labour Party*, 2nd edn, Longman.

Almond, G. and Verba, S. (1963), *The Civic Culture*, Princeton University Press.

Arblaster, A. (1984), *The Rise and Decline of Western Liberalism*, Blackwell.

Arendt, H. (1967), *The Origins of Totalitarianism*, Allen and Unwin.

Ashford, N. (1989), 'Market liberalism and the environment: a response to Hay', in *Politics*, vol. 9, no. 1.

Ayer, A. J. (1988), *Thomas Paine*, Faber and Faber.

Barker, Sir E. (1947), *Social Contract*, Oxford University Press.

Barker, M. (1975), *Gladstone and Radicalism: The reconstruction of Liberal policy in Britain 1885–94*, The Harvester Press.

Barker, R. (1978), *Political Ideas in Modern Britain*, Methuen.

Barry, N. P. (1986), *On Classical Liberalism and Libertarianism*, Macmillan.

Beer, S. H. (1982), *Modern British Politics*, 3rd edn, Faber and Faber.

Behrens, R. (1989), 'Social democracy and liberalism' in Tivey, L. and Wright, A. (eds), *Party Ideology in Britain*, Routledge.

Bell, D. (1960), *The End of Ideology*, Free Press.

Benewick, R. (1972), *The Fascist Movement in Britain*, 2nd edn, Allen Lane.

Benn, T. (1980), *Arguments for Socialism*, Penguin.

Bentley, M. (1984), *Politics Without Democracy*, Fontana.

Bentley, M. (1987), *The Climax of Liberal Politics: British liberalism in theory and practice, 1869–1918*, Edward Arnold.

Berlin, I. (1967), 'Two concepts of liberty' in Quinton, A. (ed.), *Political Philosophy*, Oxford University Press.

Bernstein, G. L. (1986), *Liberalism and Liberal Politics in Edwardian England*, Allen and Unwin.

Blake, R. (1966), *Disraeli*, Eyre and Spottiswoode.

Blake, R. (1985), *The Conservative Party from Peel to Thatcher*, Fontana.

Blunkett, D. and Jackson, K. (1987), *Democracy in Crisis*, Hogarth Press.

Boddy, M. and Fudge, C. (1984), *Local Socialism*, Macmillan.

Bosanquet, N. (1983), *After the New Right*, Heinemann.

Bradley, I. (1985), *The Strange Rebirth of Liberal Britain*, Chatto and Windus.

Bruce, S. (1987), 'Ulster loyalism and religiosity', in *Political Studies*, vol. xxxv no. 4.

Buck. P. W. (1975), *How Conservatives Think*, Penguin.

Bulpitt, J. (1987), 'Thatcherism as statecraft', in Burch, M. and Moran, M. (eds), *British Politics: A reader*, Manchester University Press.

Callaghan, J. (1987), *The Far Left in British Politics*, Basil Blackwell.

Callaghan, J. (1990), *Socialism in Britain*, Basil Blackwell.

Carsten, F. L. (1967), *The Rise of Fascism*, Batsford.

Carter, A. (1988), *The Politics of Women's Rights*, Longman.

Challinor, R. (1977), *The Origins of British Bolshevism*, Croom Helm.

Charvet, J. (1982), *Feminism*, Dent.

Clarke, J., Cochrane, A. and Smart, C. (1987), *Ideologies of Welfare*, Hutchinson.

Clarke, P. F. (1971), *Lancashire and the New Liberalism*, Cambridge University Press.

Coates, D. (1980), *Labour in Power?*, Longman.

Cowling, M. (ed.) (1978), *Conservative Essays*, Cassell.

Cranston, M. (1967), *Freedom*, 3rd edn, Longman.

Crick, B. (1987), *Socialism*, Open University Press.

Crosland, C. A. R. (1956), *The Future of Socialism*, Jonathan Cape.

Crossman, R. H. S. (1981), *The Backbench Diaries of Richard Crossman*, Morgan, J. (ed.), Hamish Hamilton and Jonathan Cape.

Cust, R. and Hughes, A. (1989), *Conflict in Early Stuart England*, Longman.

Dahrendorf, R. (1990), *Reflections on the Revolution in Europe*, Chatto and Windus.

Dangerfield, G. (1970), *The Strange Death of Liberal England*, Paladin Books.

Dearlove, J. and Saunders, P. (1984), *Introduction to British Politics*, Polity Press.

Dickens, A. G. (1959), *Thomas Cromwell and the English Reformation*, English Universities Press.

Dickinson, H. T. (1985), *British Radicalism and the French Revolution*, Basil Blackwell.

Dinwiddy, J. (1989), *Bentham*, Oxford University Press.

Disraeli, B. (1844), *Coningsby*, Penguin edn, 1983.

Disraeli, B. (1845), *Sybil*, Penguin edn, 1980.

Donald, J. and Hall, S. (eds) (1986), *Politics and Ideology*, Open University Press.

Downs, A. (1957), *An Economic Theory of Democracy*, Harper and Row.
Drucker, H., Dunleavy, P., Gamble, A. and Peele, G. (1983), *Developments in British Politics*, Macmillan.
Drucker, H., Dunleavy, P., Gamble, A. and Peele, G. (1986), *Developments in British Politics II*, Macmillan.
Dunn, J. (1969), *The Political Thought of John Locke*, Cambridge University Press.
Eccleshall, R. (1977), 'English conservatism as ideology' in *Political Studies*, vol. xxv, no. 1.
Eccleshall, R. (1986), *British Liberalism: Liberal thought from the 1640s to the 1980s*, Longman.
Eccleshall, R. (1990), *English Conservatism since the Reformation: An introduction and anthology*, Unwin Hyman.
Eccleshall, R., Geoghegan, V., Jay, R. and Wilford, R. (1984), *Political Ideologies: An introduction*, Hutchinson.
Edgar, D. (1984), 'Bitter harvest', in Curran, J. (ed.), *The Future of the Left*, Polity Press/New Socialist.
Elton, G. R. (1953), *The Tudor Revolution in Government*, Cambridge University Press.
Ensor, R. C. K. (1936), *England 1870–1914*, Oxford University Press.
Evans, B. (1984), 'Political ideology and its role in recent British politics', in Robins, L. (ed.), *Updating British Politics*, The Politics Association.
Finer, S. E. (1970), *The Life and Times of Edwin Chadwick*, Barnes and Noble.
Finer, S. E. (ed.) (1975), *Adversary Politics*, Wigram.
Firestone, S. (1979), *The Dialectic of Sex*, The Women's Press.
Flew, A. (ed.) (1979), *A Dictionary of Philosophy*, Pan/Macmillan.
Foot, M. and Kramnick, I. (eds) (1987), *The Thomas Paine Reader*, Penguin.
Foote, G. (1986), *The Labour Party's Political Thought*, Croom Helm.
Fraser, D. (1984), *The Evolution of the British Welfare State*, Macmillan.
Freeden, M. (1978), *The New Liberalism: An ideology of social reform*, Oxford University Press.
Freeden, M. (1986), *Liberalism Divided; A study in British political thought 1914–1939*, Oxford University Press.
Fukuyama, F. (1990), 'Forget Iraq – history is dead', *The Guardian*, 7 September.
Gamble, A. (1974), *The Conservative Nation*, Routledge and Kegan Paul.
Gamble, A. (1988), *The Free Economy and the Strong State*, Macmillan.
George, V. and Wilding, P. (1980), *The Ideology of Social Welfare*, Routledge and Kegan Paul.
Gilmour, I. (1978), *Inside Right*, Quartet Books.
Glasgow University Media Group (1976), *Bad News*, Routledge.
Glasgow University Media Group (1982), *Really Bad News*, Writers' and Readers' Publishing Co-operative Society.
Goodwin, B. (1982), *Using Political Ideas*, Wiley.
Gray, J. (1986), *Liberalism*, Open University Press.

Gray, R. (1981), *The Aristocracy of Labour in Nineteenth-Century Britain c. 1850–1914*, Macmillan.

Green, D. G. (1987), *The New Right*, Harvester Wheatsheaf.

Green, T. H. (1881) *Lectures on the Principles of Political Obligation*, Harris, P. and Morrow, J. (eds) (1986), Cambridge University Press.

Greenleaf, W. H. (1973), 'The character of modern British conservatism', in Benwick, R., Berki, R. N. and Parekh, B. (eds), *Knowledge and Belief in Politics*, Allen and Unwin.

Greenleaf, W. H. (1983), *The British Political Tradition, Vol. I, The Rise of Collectivism, Vol. II, The Ideological Heritage*, Methuen.

Greer, G. (1970), *The Female Eunuch*, MacGibbon and Kee.

Hall, S. (1986), 'Variants of liberalism' in Donald, J. and Hall, S. (eds), *Politics and Ideology*, Open University Press.

Hall, S. and Jacques, M. (eds) (1983), *The Politics of Thatcherism*, Lawrence and Wishart.

Hamilton, M. B. (1987), 'The elements of the concept of ideology' in *Political Studies*, vol. xxxv, no. 1, March.

Harrison, W. (1965), *Conflict and Compromise: History of British political thought*, The Free Press/Collier-Macmillan.

Hattersley, R. (1987), *Choose Freedom: The future of democratic socialism*, Michael Joseph.

Hay, J. R. (1983), *The Origins of the Liberal Welfare Reforms, 1906–1914*, Macmillan.

Hay, P. R. (1988), 'Ecological values and western political traditions from anarchism to fascism', in *Politics*, vol. 8, no. 1.

Hayek, F. P. (1975), 'The principles of a Liberal social order' in Crespigny, A. and Cronin, J. (eds), *Ideologies of Politics*, Oxford University Press.

Hayek, F. A. (1976), *The Road to Serfdom*, Routledge and Kegan Paul.

Hill, B. W. (1975), *Edmund Burke on Government, Politics and Society*, Fontana/Harvester Press.

Hill, C. (1980), *The Century of Revolution*, Van Nostrand Reinhold (International).

Hindess, B. (1971), *The Decline of Working Class Politics*, MacGibbon and Kee.

Hobhouse, L. T. (1911), *Liberalism*, with a new introduction by A. P. Grimes (1964), Oxford University Press.

Hobhouse, L. T. (1918), *The Metaphysical Theory of the State*, Macmillan.

Hobsbawm, E. (1969), *Industry and Empire*, Penguin.

Hobsbawm, E. (1989), *Politics for a Rational Left*, Verso.

Hogg, Q. (Lord Hailsham) (1947), *The Case for Conservatism*, reprinted as *The Conservative Case* (1959), Penguin.

Holland, S. K. (1975), *The Socialist Challenge*, Quartet Books.

Honderich, T. (1990), *Conservatism*, Hamish Hamilton.

Hume, L. J. (1981), *Bentham and Bureaucracy*, Cambridge University Press.

Hutton, W. (1986), *The Revolution that Never Was*, Longman.

Jacobs, B. D. (1988), *Racism in Britain*, Christopher Helm.

Jennings, Sir I. (1966), *The Law and the Constitution*, 6th edn, University of London Press.

Joseph, K. (1976), *Stranded on the Middle Ground*, Centre for Policy Studies.

Kavanagh, D. (ed.) (1982), *The Politics of the Labour Party*, Allen and Unwin.

Kedourie, E. (1960), *Nationalism*, Hutchinson.

Keegan, W. (1984), *Mrs Thatcher's Economic Experiment*, Allen Lane.

Kemp, P. and Wall, D. (1990), *A Green Manifesto for the 1990s*, Penguin.

Kirk, R. (1982), *The Portable Conservative Reader*, Viking Penguin.

King, D. S. (1987), *The New Right*, Macmillan.

Kogan, D. and Kogan, M. (1982), *The Battle for the Labour Party*, Kogan Page.

Laqueur, W. (ed.) (1979), *Fascism: A reader's guide*, Penguin Books.

Laybourn, K. (1988), *The Rise of Labour*, Edward Arnold.

Layton-Henry, Z. (1984), *The Politics of Race in Britain*, Allen and Unwin.

Layton-Henry, Z. and Rich, P. B. (eds) (1986), *Race, Government and Politics in Britain*, Macmillan.

Levitas, R. (ed.) (1986), *The Ideology of the New Right*, Polity Press.

Lichtheim, G. (1970), *A Short History of Socialism*, Weidenfeld and Nicolson.

Locke, J. (1689) *A Letter Concerning Toleration*, Gough, J. W. (ed.) (1966), 3rd edn (with *Second Treatise of Civil Government*), Basil Blackwell.

Locke, J. (1690), *Second Treatise on Civil Government*, reprinted with introduction by E. Barker (1947), Oxford University Press.

Mackenzie, J. M. (ed.) (1986), *Imperialism and Popular Culture*, Manchester University Press.

McKenzie, R. T. (1963), *British Political Parties*, 2nd edn, Heinemann.

McKenzie, R. T. and Silver, A. (1968), *Angels in Marble*, Heinemann.

McLennan, D. (1976), *Karl Marx*, Paladin, Granada Publishing.

McLennan, D. (1986), *Ideology*, Open University Press.

Macpherson, C. B. (1962), *The Political Theory of Possessive Individualism*, Oxford University Press.

Manning, D. J. (1976), *Liberalism*, Dent.

Marx, K. *Selected Writings*, McLennan, D. (ed.) (1977), Oxford University Press.

Marx, K. and Engels, F. (1880), *Selected Works* (in 2 vols), Lawrence and Wishart (1962), vol. 2, p. 127.

Michels, R. (1949), *Political Parties*, The Free Press.

Miliband, R. (1972), *Parliamentary Socialism*, 2nd edn, Merlin Press.

Mill, J. S. (1848), *Principles of Political Economy*, reprinted with introduction by D. Winch (1985), Penguin.

Mill, J. S. (1859), *On Liberty*, with introduction by M. Warnock (1962), Collins.

Mill, J. S. (1861), *Utilitarianism*, with introduction by M. Warnock (1962), Collins.

Mill, J. S. (1861), 'Representative Government', in *On Liberty, Representative Government, the subjection of Women: Three Essays* (1971), new edn, Oxford University Press.

Millett, K. (1977), *Sexual Politics*, Virago.

Minkin, L. (1978), *The Labour Party Conference*, Allen Lane.

Minogue, K. R. (1967), *Nationalism*, Batsford.

Morris, W. (1962), *Selected Writings and Designs*, Briggs, A. (ed.), Penguin.

Nairn, T. (1981), *The Break-Up of Britain*, NLB and Verso.

Newton, K. (1969), *The Sociology of British Communism*, Allen Lane.

Nisbet, R. (1986), *Conservatism*, Open University Press.

Oakeshott, M. (1962), *Rationalism in Politics and other Essays*, Methuen.

O'Sullivan, N. (1976), *Conservatism*, Dent.

Paine, T. (1791–2), *The Rights of Man*, edited with an introduction by H. Collins (1969), Penguin.

Parkin, F. (1972), *Class, Inequality and Political Order*, Paladin, Granada Publishing.

Pelling, H. (1965), *The Origins of the Labour Party*, Oxford University Press.

Pearson, R. and Williams, G. (1984), *Political Thought and Public Policy in the Nineteenth Century*, Longman.

Pierson, S. (1973), *Marxism and the Origins of British Socialism*, Cornell University Press.

Pimlott, B. (1977), *Labour and the Left in the 1930s*, Cambridge University Press.

Plumb, J. H. (1966), *The Growth of Political Stability in England*, Macmillan.

Pois, R. A. (1986), *National Socialism and the Religion of Nature*, Croom Helm.

Popper, K. R. (1962), *The Open Society and its Enemies*, 4th edn, 2 vols, Routledge and Kegan Paul.

Porritt, J. and Winner, D. (1988), *The Coming of the Greens*, Fontana.

Punnett, R. M. (1987), *British Government and Politics*, 5th edn, Gower.

Quinton, A. (1978), *The Politics of Imperfection*, Faber and Faber.

Rawls, J. (1971), *A Theory of Justice*, Harvard University Press.

Riddell, P. (1983), *The Thatcher Government*, Martin Robertson.

Rowbotham, S. (1973), *Hidden from History: 300 years of women's oppression and the fight against it*, Pluto Press.

Royle, E. (1986), *Chartism*, Longman.

St John-Stevas, N. (1982), 'Tory philosophy – a personal view' in *Three Banks Review*, June, no. 134.

Schultz, H. J. (1972), *English Liberalism and the State: Individualism or collectivism*, Heath.

Schumpeter, J. A. (1943), *Capitalism, Socialism and Democracy*, Allen and Unwin.

Scruton, R. (1980), *The Meaning of Conservatism*, Macmillan.

Scruton, R. (1983), *A Dictionary of Political Thought*, Macmillan/Pan.

Seldon, A. (ed.) (1990), *UK Political Parties since 1945*, Philip Allan.

Seliger, M. (1976), *Ideology and Politics*, Allen and Unwin.
Seyd, P. (1987), *The Rise and Fall of the Labour Left*, Macmillan.
Seymour-Ure, C. (1974), *The Political Impact of the Mass Media*, Constable.
Smith, A. (1776), *The Wealth of Nations*, edited with introduction by E. Cannan (1976), University of Chicago Press.
Smith, P. (1967), *Disraelian Conservatism and Social Reform*, Routledge.
Solomos, J. (1986), 'Trends in the political analysis of racism' in *Political Studies*, vol. XXXIV, no. 2.
Spencer, H. (1969), *The Man Versus the State*, Penguin.
Talmon, J. L. (1960), *The Origins of Totalitarian Democracy*, Praeger.
Tawney, R. H. (1921), *The Acquisitive Society*, Fontana.
Tawney, R. H. (1931), *Equality*, new edn (1964), Unwin.
Tawney, R. H. (1938), *Religion and the Rise of Capitalism*, Penguin.
Taylor, S. (1982), *The National Front In English Politics*, Macmillan.
Thatcher, M. (1977), *Let Our Children Grow Tall*, Centre for Policy Studies.
Thompson, E. P. (1980), *The Making of the English Working Class*, Penguin.
Thompson, K. (1986), *Beliefs and Ideology*, Ellis Horwood and Tavistock Publications.
Thurlow, R. C. (1986), *Fascism in Britain: A history 1918–1985*, Basil Blackwell.
Tivey, L. (ed.) (1981), *The Nation State*, Martin Robertson.
Tivey, L. and Wright, A. (1989), *Party Ideology in Britain*, Routledge.
Vincent, J. (1966), *The Formation of the Liberal Party 1857–1868*, Constable.
Watson, J. S. (1960), *The Reign of George III*, Oxford University Press.
Wuldegruve, W. (1978), *The Binding of Leviathan*, Hamish Hamilton.
Weatherall, D. (1976), *David Ricardo*, Martinus Nijhoff.
Whiteley, P. (1983), *The Labour Party in Crisis*, Methuen.
Williams, R. (1976), *Keywords*, Fontana/Croom Helm.
Wollstonecraft, M. (1792), *A Vindication of the Rights of Women*, Brody, M. (ed.) (1982), Penguin.
Wright, A. (1983), *British Socialism*, Longman.
Wright, D. G. (1970), *Democracy and Reform, 1815–1885*, Longman.
Young, H. (1989), *One of Us*, Macmillan.

Index